A Democracy of Poisons

Also by Tim Allen

Texts for a Holy Saturday (Phlebas, 1995)
The Cruising Duct (Maquette, 1998)
Sea Ex/Change (itinerant press, 2007)
Settings (Shearsman Books, 2008)
An Anabranch with Slug (Knives Forks & Spoons Press, 2011)
incidental harvest (Oystercatcher, 2011)
The Voice Thrower (Shearsman Books, 2012)
The Carousing Duck (zimZalla, 2014)
Copyright (Department, 2014)
Tattered by Magnets (Knives Forks & Spoons Press, 2014)
Default Soul (Red Ceilings, 2914)
A New Geography of Romanticism (Red Ceilings, 2015)
Anecdotage (Dock Road Press, 2017)
Under The Cliff Like (if p then q, 2017)
Portland: a Triptych – with Norman Jope and Mark Goodwin (Knives Forks & Spoons Press, 2019)
Peasant Tower (Disengagement, 2021)

Don't Start Me Talking – with Andrew Duncan (Salt Publishing, 2006)

A Democracy of Poisons

a sequence of 100 prose poems

Tim Allen

Shearsman Books

First published in the United Kingdom in 2021 by
Shearsman Books Ltd
PO Box 4239
Swindon
SN3 9FN

Shearsman Books Ltd Registered Office
30–31 St. James Place, Mangotsfield, Bristol BS16 9JB
(this address not for correspondence)

www.shearsman.com

ISBN 978-1-84861-788-9

Copyright © Tim Allen, 2021.

The right of Tim Allen to be identified as the author of this work has been asserted by his Estate in accordance with the Copyrights, Designs and Patents Act of 1988.
All rights reserved.

ACKNOWLEDGEMENTS
Thanks to the editors of *Stride, Junction Box, International Times, Decals of Desire* and *An Educated Desire – for Robert Sheppard at 60* (Knives Forks & Spoons Press).

A Democracy of Poisons

To my friends back in Plymouth
– the Truth Brothers etc. (see pg. 101)

1. Walk

I walk into a narrative I don't run I don't crawl or creep I casually insert my self into the forest. The forest is a restroom with guessing desk and chairs from the hall. The guest demands to be the first motif to be ignored sat on all the chairs at once made of hand torn shirts but the hairs are broken and the hands are worn. I walk further into the fortress I don't run I don't call or weep I slot pages into any magazine where such stories maybe true. Empty magazines litter the forest floor.

Automata and splinters. Puffballs smash the cricket pavilion windows with golf balls thrown by slobs and goofballs. All balls stolen from the PE cupboard will be represented by a single buckyball a privileged ball of lightning lobbed onto the roof of the bandstand to trickle down to land on the path. It is now a cricket ball. Things move fast. One end of the forest grows while the other is chopped. Talk on the next table is of memory. Do not recall it. Lion on the next chair does the splits.

Automata covered in blisters do the talking not being completely plastered there is still more automata than blister resurrecting a human's chalked out bliss on a park path circling the bandstand. While hiking around this desk think *honeycomb* and *dragon* but don't run them together hold them to their promised time zones then intercept yourself in the flesh flash, a sprinter hefting a harp off the starting blocks. Yet not all splinters are wood. Some are the result of *metalwork for boys*.

Now the walk has been talking in the forest for four hours without encountering any tail. It hears glass breaking. It is extraneous. A robot is baptised by another reboot who mistrusts the native minstrel's religion and trips across a hammock strung between the desk and chair that is unstable and supports no weight no matter how empty the tale. A ball trickles towards my shoe. It is Newton's apple but I've never trusted those shoes that apple or proverbial literature in general.

2. Lunch

A lunch-break is a perfect period for time to thicken as there is enough time to take your glasses off or put your glasses on. Sometimes even time for both. There is enough space for the traffic and enough space for *you* but to stand it you have to have a ticket to not stand out. The lion has four horizons in eyes for walking on the waves. In the channel a storm is *brewing*. Extinction by degrees. In a sewage tunnel a storm is *abating*. Now there is time and space in and for a lunch-break.

A pig reads a newspaper in a cartoon. In the newspaper a pig reads a newspaper in a cartoon. Etc. This is an old story. We've heard this story before or something very much like it. The pig sits down to read the paper. Now that the newspaper is a paper the story could change radically the paper could be a letter though not a letter in a newspaper, not even this one. Time can hang heavy for pigs having to hang around in litters. Those who end badly need distraction. We all end badly.

A note is a still-life of a document's credentials. An invoice bills a will's sheet of info. Sleep posts a fan letter selfie to an A list dentist identifying himself in an identical chair. So where are your papers? Show me your passport. No, this is a restricted area, from that road over there to that park bench over there. Where you sit was a farmyard though not necessarily the actual yard. Guitars made to resonate like bagpipes are tone poems hatched half way up traffic heavy hills.

Mermaid hides her purse in the maelstrom. The city hides behind Portland stone. The purse slides behind a wastepaper basket of its own volition. Lunch-break is a type of time machine. Not a very good one. It never works. I don't think it's meant to work. Only *you* work. In bad weather it is not a very good idea to have lunch in the nearby park it is better to prop yourself in a doorway of the office block and let your mind wander where it will. Mild hunger, they say, may help this process.

3. Growing

It is growing cold. The cold grows rows of black puddings but residual hotcakes linger in the puddings long after the potlatch. We lack for no reason. Our blood sausage is made from blankets. We call out for no reason. We call on *you* for no reason after all the season is warm and if it was any larger so what, would we normally be so hot? Nobody wants that except the few who do. I feel for the very tall having to repeat themselves leafing through party talk and picking their way through the night as if there were definitely a sixpence in there somewhere.

The number of people saying they no longer believe in the benefits of progress is surprising. Do they mean it? Is it a passing fashion? Shiver me timbers. I suppose it's one way of looking at things. Everything shakes apart from a brave few who roll so do you think it's still OK to feel sorry for yourself when stood outside *ones' self* looking in or does that remove any real reason for feeling sorry in the first place? Indeed, sometimes I agree with John Gray about stuff, but not always, no.

Me and my pharaoh walking down the avenue want to kill the enemy but should we start the job or finish it off in our own street? The avenue grows rows, threats of repeated *kick offs*, the tension in the room plucked from the air by a chair leg clumsily slotted crookedly fast by a budget poltergeist. When a tree has a devilish guardian this is the result. When my dog is disturbed I smooth her. She loves the smoothing to be repeated later when there is no longer any disturbing residue.

What would happen if everyone had their own personal path through the forest leading to a communal well being and what if we all had joints that could swell and contract like boards in a rowing boat adrift in clouds drunk from a bucket of foreign body rain? Yes some people are held together by glue but some have to be nailed together. That could be read wrongly but it could also be read rightly.

4. Picture

Picture this please: a black and white colour film. If the image is hanging its head is it a dead sunflower? Go on picture it. It is now an order an imperative of the kind America makes in war films. They make a lot of those one way or another. You can learn a lot from films yet often it is not what the film makers intended. They wanted to teach you manners. I think we can call them *manners* it's what they amount to. Now a pickled sun jammed in brown sky looks critically squiffy.

The patch of sunflowers is meant to evoke sunflower fields as far as the horizon. The tarry face lends a sticky hand to lifeboat heroes who are now men mending the road in need of that hand to upgrade the motorway or, to put it another way, to save a popular and successful TV drama from being seen by millions more you need the support and wonderful weirdness of the little birds hopping around in a denuded winter hedge. If it was summer sunny you would see their silhouettes.

Sometimes bird shaped leaves in the hedge are actually egg shaped and amusing yet we are always too ready to leave such pictures behind and land like a fly on others. We can be stupid. Only when a bird is acting stupid does it resemble us in any discernible way and you must have seen it sung e.g. *the wind cries Mary* – no stop being soft Jimi when people say stuff we picture it e.g. a prisoners' concert party requiring varieties of uniform to amuse rank masses and the shadows of soldiers wearing uniforms that should be reserved for pompous circumstances.

A sketch of sunflowers picks up the kids from school. A black and white jaundice sells feathers as picturesque as a crisp new packet of tobacco. The blanket that the *Indian* wraps himself in is the same blanket he uses to make smoke signals. It's obvious. It makes economic sense. When it is summer sunny the darkness in the hedge thickens the gravy making it difficult to observe what you are hearing.

5. Objects

Objects allowed back in the story grow new claws. Clause now behaves itself it does this by thinking of others. Good cause. Because he's been in the forest now for forty days and fifteen thrifty nights without spying from behind trees maybe he is only into rejected images walking through walls jaw dropping but no Jesus lies behind miscalculated Jesuit angles and a subversive guide-book we stop to scrutinize from memory. Nevertheless pausing halfway down a page he collides with a flying man. A superhero? No, this object no superhero. No such thing mate.

Excuses we make to ourselves are hugged tightly in sorrow caught in a bathroom mirror wider and longer than the bathroom in which it hangs. These houses we *make unto ourselves* are pop-up mermaids in a Pre-Raphaelite gambit led by dog-ends into the dark dusk of an allotment. What's your excuse for finding yourself here? I am looking for the benefit gig but have forgotten who is playing and who for. I've lost two dogs here but neither are the source of this ramshackle mystery.

Strewth, more rhymes based on old photos. They're not mine I don't write those sort my compositions are of milky seashells and strips of tasteless wallpaper by which I mean the wallpaper tastes as you would expect it to, wood mixed with a blend of sour sugars. Dying man staring at a wallpaper book has to decide on an infinity to want. Will he opt for sea dogs' memories giving anemones a new angle or one based on personality tests premised on an individual's taste in wallpaper?

The clawed back objects outlive us anyway but I could never grasp the appeal of superheroes. I didn't mind Zorro, he was OK. I didn't mind Robin Hood either or Wulf the Briton but I was young that's my excuse. I have other excuses too but you won't hear them from me I leave such things to the songstress in distress singing The Leaving of Liverpool in the Devonport folk club *A Lesbian's First Kiss.*

6. Normal

It was a normal room. It is still a normal room. Tomorrow it will be abnormal in a backwash of Feng Shui mistakes. *We all make mistakes* is what we people say yet there are some supermen types who never make 'em and I bet you those freakish folk still say *we all make mistakes*. They are not being disingenuous they are just being taken a tad too literally. I wouldn't put any money on it though. That would be a huge mistake. I do make mistakes but no I wouldn't make room for that one.

The room was furnished with the fashions of another country's history or that's how it seemed. The room was done-out, it was *furn-ish-ed* with a table made with bad light thrown out with the century old tin bathwater. The chairs were rotting corpses, beds organised as if for war, yet a pall of conventionality hung over the bric-a-brac making it a routine room. One could live there quite comfortably for a moment or two. If every room makes a statement then yes, this was Baby's room.

They returned to the room soon after dark and set up camp in the...... No, sorry, they didn't, not without camping gear. They returned by dusk and planted their bicycles next to the water butt. But they didn't did they I bet they did not? They planted their bicycles in the desert whereabouts drawer of the extendable table. Soon it will be harvest – reminisce before it is too late. We were taking a big risk fleeing early from that expendable house auction by driving down rutted fields.

On running back to the new moors the cyclists sat around the table eating tripe and talking shop. The table was not really round as these were not real knights just laminated birthday bumps in the larynxes and oesophagi of executed norms. At night these tubes of ectoplasm emerge to make fun of an invited audience of hardware shopkeepers, the purveyors of pressure cooker parts and *families of brushes*. Strong polish normally hides the corruption under creased green baize.

7. Tunnel

The tunnel. The escape tunnel. The tunnel branched from hut to hut in a maze it didn't creep it didn't run it inserted itself, a Planet Earth in a plangent mirroring. That sounds sound. Mirroring without light needs little repeating in the *cold light of day*. Another old tale. Time hangs but not for our Chaplain for this indefinite divine gift-aids us salvation in packets so some prisoners are digging a tunnel of love. What kind of soil is removed from such business and where is it deposited?

I lent my favourite book to a man in another hut. I am waiting for him to give it back. I lent it to him at least an hour ago. Time goes slowly here. The book was a gift from my wife and is the only thing I can call my own in this community. It is called *The Aesthetics of Glass* and is all about a bloke who meets a woman who is wearing a dress decorated with cuttlefish. It's a love story I suppose even though, to be frank, there is little love in it. The chap spends all his money on Chaplain's meditation classes and the poor lass ends up being committed to the aquarium.

Beyond the prison camp there is a forest. This forest can be sensed. It is not to be sneezed at. We can hear many birds. The birds are free thinkers but I know that's just a fancy. Wolves dump their dead at the gates of the camp where some grey men imagine they are being wolves but they are quite wrong as they are nothing like any wolves I know. Beyond the forest villages burn. Farms burn. Unabashed. By the way *The Aesthetics of Glass* has rich transparencies that keep crinkling up.

Yes this film is a dumping ground for escapist fancies. The Director doesn't even deserve his title. The Commandant deserves his title more than him because at least the Commandant commands. He commands respect. I like to think I give that respect freely because the heart is a fast confluence of diverse emotions and disturbing motives. The Commandant has learned much from his few mistakes.

8. Study

The Study was turned into a room. November is curious to know what December has in store for it. The year end is a hanging time of excavated ideas and shallow side dishes. The libido turned to the ego and said *shut that bloody door* while the children played being horses careering around the field and jumping fences but they didn't really career around a field they careered around the room and then didn't jump fences but hopped over atmosphere and not one of them would have a career in dressage though in years to come would definitely jockey for position.

Seconds pass. Long seconds of shuffled thought. Applause tentatively begins then *grows* then explodes in a firework display of burning confetti and theatre tickets. Rows fill with brides and aisles with bridles. Horses will never know the children were copying them. Their own seconds pass. Time snags. Horses *hold their heads* in a perfect balance of human gloom and animal confidentiality as a fine likeness of a horse sizzles onto paper (tambourine sound) sweating like helicopter flanks in that sallow old yellow Vietnamese newsreel. The copter makes a second pass.

Solstice monotonous rocking horse talk to us. The retired teacher put out to stud. Leonora Carrington came to read at Peter Barlow's Cigarette she came on a train from her father's Lancastrian mansion as amongst its aristocratic bric-a-brac and tack a toy railway station grew from a *strapping young man's* saddle. On arrival at the Town Hall Tavern she painted us a skunk trap then made a pass at the skunk.

A joyrider merges with the M1060 but unlike him Leonora speaks for the whole herd creeping past the Study door then careering down the corridor to *his* room that carries an echo of a singular career spent air tunnelling towards escalating tinnitus and mental cramp. The Study is rarely used these days for *the passage of time*. It's questions short of problems. The dust gathering there no longer human.

9. Other

Other people begin novels the way best friends end their poems. I believe this is worth saying even though it is probably not true not if you were to actually look and compare but nobody is going to look and compare or notice my unwritten novels ending the way others beg for oblivion. All other people are novels except for a few walking about you might class as poems. Wasn't that worth waiting for?

Street and forest in equal measure. Breathing sculptures sigh *there's nothing in it, far too easy to make our tough arty cocoons crease crack and crumple under the pressure of the so easily accessible.* I've no idea about art. Art is a monarch's pile of unwanted gifts from the kings of other lands. If that's not worth saying then by implication there should be no comparing disabilities or street food posh nosh.

Forest struggled out of the street. Street struggled out of the trees. I've been in a few posh restaurants well posh for Plymouth I no longer live in Plymouth but I can't prove it, never knew I had to. The forest struggled into the street. The street struggled into the restaurant. Other people lived on Plymouth roads and still do so go and interview them. I left it once but later once I left it I thought I might *end up* writing about it at last but not while struggling to read in St. Helens Library.

Shockwave charm alarm clocked *waving not drawing* on a big sheet of invisible paper. Is that funny? Was it worth asking? A phantom limb pain no longer knows which arm of the law it is only what others think it's for. A bit basic to count as a philosophy but it wasn't lawyers who invented thinking so let it pass. Rhetorical questions are the ones worth answering but to be honest that's because they're lifted from the myriad of answers to writers' block. It's a struggle reading others especially when there's no books not even with a stamped skew-whiff *Cancelled*. The rugged charm of other writers' hovels begins at the threshold of this palace.

10. Name

Name a current TV game show please tell us what is going on in your life. No one need be maimed by embarrassment just for designing labels for a *Label Design Magazine*. Post-modernity and the past go in the toilets at Plymouth Argyle from different ends by which is meant different ends of the toilets not different ends of the ground. These are *ends* because the crowd crush (yes we did get crowds at Home Park, in the toilets anyway) made it impossible to tell entrance from exit. You had to look for signs lurking behind a swaying sea of heads and shoulders *if so inclined*. It din't matter none. It don't matter not really – mattered by tangents.

Pointless! Trying to write Christmas cards but slowed down in the annual task by forgetting the names of poets' partners. Syria, what a lovely name for a beach. An octave drops. Temperatures surface glass ceilings thicken and metaphors freeze. Only when metonymy breaks the monotony do flowers *wilt also*. *The Chase* is on. A novelist trashed his repute by throwing his hotel room out of the window. His secretary followed. A swimming pool full of rock stars' blood was waiting for her.

All objects have souls. Does saying that imply having a fertile imagination or is it too obvious to say because it is not true? Objects have souls but barren subjects do not so if one (one? good Lord!) is both object and subject flickering between both in a *special effect* does *one* have a soul or the promise of one? Or does a soul have a forest to type all its questions? Can a soul *land a good job* like a secretary?

The name stitched onto the school shoe bag said *Hanging Judge*. Later different names went shebang on the duffel bag *namely* Rimbaud, Baudelaire & Mallarmé. The class fleabag was also the school fleabag because kids can be educated out of becoming art students as portrayed by a neutral observer who isn't quite himself today and isn't anyone else either. Today he's haggling with death, in shorthand.

11. Interested

I am not interested in words I am only interested in myself so I insert myself into others' stories then look for myself as if I was Wally. I can never find Wally. I am reasonably interested in what words do though e.g. *the wordless windmill* they are not interested in what I do though e.g. *worthy miller Deft-as-a-Post* walking *atop* a waterfall with Escaped Prisoner climbing an Alp without any feeling in his fingers knows full well that all feelings will return when they punish his heresy.

An Airfix model of the Marie Celeste *sits* on a bedside cupboard. The pieces were not glued together by that little tube of glue they were glued together by that tub of sailor's semen that *sits* on the bedside table. Don't touch! Don't sit on the table. Don't sit on after the meal has finished. Don't stand on ceremony. You may pick the model up as long as you don't lift it. It may well fall apart in your dreams.

The Fall play it for laughs in the British Legion Hut on Portland. My dad gets up to dance with another man'*s old lady* he picked up tickets for the dance in a pack of superhero cards that use the shower cubicle for a toilet. The band encore with *The March of the Contrarians* warming-up for Hearsay playing in a working men's club in Stoke, Plymouth. Hitching once I was picked up by a Stoker but I couldn't tell from his accent which Titanic film we were drowning in. Hearsay open with a punishing version of *Come Together* to a right shower of Gothic Bran/d Flakes.

Airfix were not the only model makers there was another brand you had to make yourself called Revell and I had to make myself do it to prove I was a boy because girls were bred to model clothes and not interested in words except words about them which tended to escape through an icy tunnel in a fire storm of objectified fear. Maybe. Maybe baby. Gluey words from love letters wearing their underwear shimmy up the wrecked ship's mast that lies jammed the length of the waterfall.

12. Fictional

Fictional sky. Fictional trees. Fictional man. From the pits of disappointment to the heights of great fiction. Fictional grey of deep winter sky blankets the world in more mirrors than there is deeply diffused grey light coalescing into the form of another fictional man acting as a witness. Two real men who will never meet nod to each other on the road that borders the forest. A muffled *alright?* from one of them is answered almost simultaneously with a croaked *OK* from the other.

I really do believe that the objects we share our lives with can read our thoughts without possessing any language *as such*. Only by saying that *I really do believe* can I emphasise the muscular control that these objects exert over the direction of my thoughts. It has nothing to do with fiction fantasy or realist it is to do with close-up injections including *affairs of the heart* that can blast all belief systems.

Conceptual gentleness in entangled shadows. Tight fitting genre streams and the loose living tensions of unidentified objects floating down those same streams. Standing on a bridge and looking down at the water is a person of indeterminate gender they (yes *they*) play with the notion that all talk about distant exoplanets is nonsense that astronomy could be replaced by Portland Sheep illuminated by white lightening. This figure on a bridge figures in many well-known paintings.

A ribcage is measured for a costume drama before the mirror. The mirror has to wait. The sky cracks like ribs head butted by a little lad not watching where he's going he's just run out of school in Tottenham in 1973 all keyed up in the garish dark blue and dirty red dyes of an ancient Punk zine used to identify a rare breed of sheep – dark blue for the border between reality and fiction and red for a road between forest and sky. The road runs parallel with a watery ditch you are saved from by a Stats and Probability student but nothing can save you from his pity.

13. Step

Step back. Look how an alien structure emerges from familiar details. Step even further back. See how well you can scarcely see the scattered seeds and clods of meteorite. Now turn and look at the structure again. Tell what you see. In even steps the Complaints Department shrinks while Public Relations take over room after room from which spokesmen and Pokémon women poke forth & multiply. Now retrace your steps while the familiar structure breaks up into alien details.

Fresh from the shower re-fleshed from the pornographic flower shop a chalet slips down a fresh cliff fall and lies facedown on the rocks of Jesus of the Beach. On the shingle. On the sand. Facedown. Facedown the shower door to the shop is a window in the windowless irritation of the tide-line or the aging enemy within. I heard the miners that *enemy within* the Earth wring out carbon fresh from the local shower. Double agent steps sheepishly from the little theatre voting booth.

Prudence puts recipe for vertigo back on the high shelf and floods batteries in a shower of hot ash from *the crater by the gate*. The postman's terminal man in a van's discreet progress races Zeno's arrow to addresses in his customer file. The lock on the nearby canal never stops filling. I feel sick. Are these the heights of *non-fiction*? The distant look on a distant canal never stops emptying into a Japan shaped like the British Isles. Step away Judge. Oh how healthy is our democracy!

Step up and marvel at the cheap Americana. Look! See! The creator by the park gate digs out a muddy battery instead of a flint. Giggled sparks light-up a parked postal coach collecting Christmas cards from the lock-keeper's complaints box. Look! – a horse-drawn mask facedown on the rocks. See! A black cat tied-up with white elastic dancing *atop* the town wall. Look! – see the masque follow the wall around the waist of a column of ants carrying a used car battery *beyond the pale*.

14. Bronchial

Bronchial tributaries. Tracks crisscrossing through the forest. Canoe racks and wood turned grubs. Pallets of slime and grubby goblins turning in their graves of liquefied liquorice. Chronic fiction of acute facts piles clouds higher as if hiring an invisible tit-for-tat hat above the roar of birdcage jets choking on chewed worms instead of partying with the unattributed *Fulcrum & Educational Hierarchy* band.

The dance begins in the face in imperceptible muscle flex. The dancer practises when left alone with the moves but now he must let movement speak and give movement a voice but maybe it doesn't want a voice maybe it'd rather just twitch far beneath us in seismic narcissism yet see how the moves flow now see how they run the gamut of mental landscaping. The dancer bleeds from every orifice.

Irate narrator loses track so considers hiring one of those irritating shortest story ever competitions that just produce bad haiku to crisscross cracks across the estate's scull where a man carrying two plastic bags of shopping is wound-up. The bags are light but he would love them to be heavy one half of him would rather drag them he passes a shortest story ever told but cannot read it. He saps. He is sapped, a stale fridge bulging with bad air and leaking bones but when he gets back to his flat he will put the radio on and listen for more lines to *plunder*.

Why does what they call high modernism have so much religion bronchial hymns and ripped sacking in it? Modernised slavery modernised piracy the streets treat the fields to spa town poverty. Pirate Radio is no longer leaking from every office anyway the face has more than its fair share of orifices so tell me dear how did you wind-up here? Did you stick to a track? How did you cross the forest without possessing any of the forester's skills? Look! See! The DJ's mobile home waiting in a lay-by. I take it you have come to interview this vampire before he wakes.

15. Saying

Saying the least tramps over a 3D map of blood spatter that follows you home on an open top bus. The past is catching up *to say the least*. The esplanade is sprayed with rays of lemonade light stubbornly in love with a seaside town getting uglier every year. A ramp up. Access. A bunk-up at least. The drawbridge to Paradise is actually the road that skirts it. Paradise begins down there in the water that runs beneath the bridge. White swans in the black water. A Children's Crusade river.

Shut up Clive James. Shut up Stephen Fry. Shut your mouth Jonathan Ross. Put a sock in it Chris Evans. My army is full of hatred for you all you are all a bunch of gits. To say the least. Lord Byron got me into trouble once it was all down to his maiden speech to the House of Lords 'cause I didn't read it properly *to be honest* I didn't read it at all I had to write an essay on it but couldn't be arsed so wrote a piece of automatics (called *Cricket*) that dressed the Virgin Mary *up* in bright red.

Articulate wolf waits to be spoken to by the guards at the camp gate. One guard shoulders his rifle and picks up a stone the other guard hefts up his rifle to take aim. This winter triptych alone could make this war worthwhile. The guards are far from home but those they guard are even further away to say the least. They are not guarded to keep them safe from werewolves but to keep the guards' own homes safe to return to – unbeknown an entirely pointless exercise. Like school.

A city is built on the river and the marsh. Paradise is the capital of the conquered world and is a world in its own right too, a world of barges pontoons and fencing clubs gambling tables and Joy Divisions, a world where adults are not allowed in unless accompanied by a press card. Our victories *in the field* are celebrated with alcohol our victories at sea are celebrated with sex. Defeats are laborious discos of remembrance to which old soldiers are let in to do the *Dance of the Luddites*.

16. Shimmer

The shimmer on a shoulder twelve parsecs wide is the hat of an earthborn star. The hat has a nose a moustache a van and an onerous mission plus a job-lot of botched predictions. The opposing shadow on a hammer twenty-one parsecs off is the older twin of the Bang Bang system. The room is taking shape. It takes the shape of a road. You can pick the road up and hang it around your neck of the woods and you can sing or breathe but not both. It's one or the other I'm afraid.

There are an equal number of things I like and dislike about post-modernism. An example of a favourite would be the way it debunks trite wisdom while a disliked favourite would be its tendency to pick and choose values according to a current price and no that's not calling a rose a rose it is calling one a flower. When Bob Dylan made *Nashville Skyline* I predicted he would be a post-modernist and forty-five years later he proved me spot on with his Xmas album and lingerie adverts.

In the interview Bob Dylan was motionless. His mouth moved. His mouth moved in three dimensions of time and one of space. In the interview Dylan's teeth were a testament to his bemused intelligence. The chair he sat in had arms for his very arms and he used them with a sure sense of his own relativistic worth. Folklore Throne. Electric chair. Electric throne. He answered questions the way he always did with a wry take on honesty but this time the smile stayed spacewalking in the eyes, any spare words being astronomical measurements of their own refraction.

A snapshot caught a Caterpillar Galaxy nibbling fusion dust off a coffee table. The coffee table never got used for coffee but for good-natured banter between aging lefty scruffs and smart young alt-rights. A coffee table book called Exotic Galaxies lay *open upon it* at a double page Butterfly Galaxy spread. *I see you've chosen to breathe and not sing, son* said Bob. *Time will tell if you've made the correct choice.*

17. Flock

A flock of angels devoured Heaven in an hour flat. The flatness of the hour is very important here. The flock of birds regurgitated Hell in our flat – the go-slow puff of evolution minus an eternity in one room. The more rips there are in the fabric of space/time the more dusters there are – one for each knickknack in fact. Every knickknack is a rock or a fossil and a memory of the old cobbled block is carried by each. The mantelpiece they perch on is a Parisian street chunk circa May '68.

A pack of dogs is chasing a ship. The little ship is puffing up-hill. The little ship is too big to be a boat. Our vocabulary is large and useful it can describe the littlest thing by which I mean the smallest possible difference between numbers. Don't dismay, a simple book read by nobody special gallops uphill as fast as it descends the hill of *be careful what you wish for* but how to be careful when the world is a democracy of poisons it's not as if you were a roofer and had to repair a rotten roof even though from such a roof you could see as far as the grave of Max Jacob.

In our flat in Crouch End we gave a home to a hamster called Vincent. We called him Vincent because he only had one ear I think his mother must have bitten the other ear off. We bought him in a pet shop somewhere near Alexandra Palace, or at least you could see Alexandra Palace reflected in the pet shop window, high up in a bird cage. Vincent was yellowy white he was the first of our many hamsters. In that flat we also homed two zebra finches, Freddie and Freda, that loved each other as we loved each other. Our landlord and landlady loved each other as well.

And now once again it is time to remember the British war dead. The curvature of the hour is important here and even though there is nothing to say flocks eat it up as if it were *honest to goodness* bird food. *To be honest* I'd rather be one of the German war dead whom even the mother and father are not allowed to speak of.

18. Walk 2

Walk into the room don't crawl or creep keep going as if walking into a sheet stretching softly into the firmament. Half way into the forest pause and wonder how you know this is half way into the room. Snowflakes on the forest floor are 5000° celsius so don't look through a lens look straight at it around a hollow bent tree renting-out inhaled violence to chilly night via the abandoned mouth of a runaway who stops to know it's half way into the forest as understanding dawns.

The coast of Brittany talks to the coast of Cornwall in a chaos of translations that *whistle while you work*. The sea is a harvest of Chinese whispers – a medium in a mess. The mess is spick-and-span. Naval officers drift in and out with the minds of mathematicians drowning in new numbers dreamt up by a Merlin, a vibrating ink spot in a missing network of caves. Search parties sent out to search for these caves in the stubborn runaway's body let dawn extinguish the lamps then return home empty hearted down crazy paving that meanders past trapdoor horizons.

Walk the straight path don't cry or weep keep going as if it had a purpose. Sheets are for sleeping in lashed to a mast in sheets of lashing rain it is only a dream but a very clear one, its coherence a bit off-putting. A dream should unwrap on recall to reveal a hollow core that can spin itself into art but this one spits pips turning molten. Walk out of the canvas one step at a time or two at a time if you so wish.

The traffic out on the main road backs up as far as J.M.W. Turner. This grey rain dreams in coloured echoes too much like selective memory. What remains of the searchers' hope teeters in stage wings lost far out in the orchestral wings of the ocean. Supernatural draughts upend a room far too sizeable to cross with such a hopelessly modern narrative – it's a phantom twisting free from an avalanche of mucous. So stand down stubborn human heart. You no longer override alien art.

19. Cricket

A cricket pavilion in the Alps stops for a spot of lunch. The scenic panorama is of a pinch of salt crossing a lake far below in a purple paper boat. Having done with the pavilion the *view* resumes its journey down a buttercup corridor daisy cut by a cow *tucked in* two in Vivian Stanshall's burnt bed of English roses where circus tents and courtroom doors are swirled with political slogans gang tags and occult ciphers. Defaced. The hospital wards have been defaced by hooligans and clowns.

The prisoner of war hut is both en suit and circumspect. Its occupants are lolling around for the camera. Lying on my bunk I read a newspaper well actually I'm not reading it but I am looking at it. In a moment or two I will perform my lines conveying that it's a foreign newspaper probably Polish and that the edition is at least two years old. That is how long we have been here. In Limbo. I have been here a lot longer than the others actually waiting an eternity to speak my lines.

The officer nominally in charge in the hut says very little and keeps his orders to a minimum. *Use grammar correctly* when speaking to or about him is the rule he is fairly strict about. He is fair. I wouldn't say he is lax. We are fair. I wouldn't say we are lax. A mop leans casually by the hut door. The mop is a prop. We have to pretend to pretend it is a woman by calling it Daphne. Leant on the back wall is a stiff brush. We tease ourselves cruelly by pretending the brush is Daphne's lover.

A dog with a silky golden coat that shines in the sun is bounding along on gravel. The gravel turns to tarmac. A car with a silky red coat that's shining in the sun is *bombing down the road*. I'm driving in the opposite direction to pick up a piece of shabby chic that my daughter has bought *at market* when I see the tragic results of the dog *bounding* and the car *bombing*. I piece things back together. Once I was an anarchist and part of me is still optimistic when buying a charity shop jigsaw.

20. Pale

Pale lads and stale cakes. In the local news Pals Brigades make National bulletins. Stale cake sale confessional box climbs Everest taking bullets by surprise too as they enter a sea sergeant roaring *Do your places up lad or tonight you will sleep on the seabed with Charles Mintern and the Andy Jordanaires* oh yes wouldn't it be worse watching your pals being *mowed down*? wouldn't it hit home harder? Yea maybe the idea is to get you really really titanically angry. Psychological warfare.

A wormhole held the promise of adventure and death. On the *outing* I was trying to look at the landscape but then everyone started singing *One man went to mow*. We were getting closer to home, soon there would be familiar streets. The coach was probably similar to those you see in jigsaws nostalgic for the 50's. We never visited the castle on the hill but maybe that would happen on a different day-trip down Miss Liddell's wormhole wearing Granny's psychedelic specs to *save time*.

Two eloping meadows trip over stills from three different Titanic films shuffled then treated to a slap of paint which *low and behold* goes on and wins the Turner. No matter that the artist was winging it. His acceptance speech goes down a well before coming back up festooned with bladder wrack and fish bones. At The Brits tanned Bratz Dolls place purple wreaths at the foot of a cenotaph, a monument to engorgement carved in pumice and shoved in a pointe shoe shod *In Parenthesis*.

Meanwhile an erstwhile chinwag on Radio 4 about *Place* between a chap and his ashtray gets *bogged down* by in-jokes that fill up an irrigation channel with retail water that flumes to the village hall where the W.I. *cock-an-ear* when the speaker tells of her rape fantasies. The post-talk discussion gets *bogged down* in dunked biscuits and the anthropomorphic qualities of stewed tea while trapped between gigantic book-ends the landscape reneges on its contract with the poor pale lads.

21. Far

Far from a human habitation where tundra thunder echoes and eardrums freeze there is a little piece of hypocrisy that will be forever England. Everything else is finite, but not that. A gorilla hung himself. He'd been put on a charge sheet by his sergeant and he didn't like it so was making a protest making a statement but his friends said, in private, he was *making a spectacle of himself*, in private. Artificial seasons incubate far inside the dome. Temporary staff sweeping up pine needles.

There used to be these beach changing huts but changing huts without any walls. I suppose a canvas was draped over the framework. Boxes you could sit on were attached to the floor and one afternoon that's what we did my girlfriend and me and Eddie and his. We *reclined* looking at a Saturday sky. The huts started where Weymouth sand changed into Greenhill shingle. I preferred walking the shingle's crisp deep crunch in much the same way I preferred Eddie's girlfriend to mine.

The difference between asteroids and meteors, I read, is down to location. When far from human habitation a room remembers human habits and finds a place to sleep in an American expat's book of Parisian verse. It snuggles in but when it wakes there is nothing civilised for breakfast and though *Room* may very well fall absently in love with the closest to hand page in the book this location's not that conducive for long-term survival. If it stays another night it might well *burn up*.

The forest too is burning up. The forest has a fever. It is walking the streets as if they were a Frenchman far from France. Room has a fever too, one that kills time and cheats death by hanging itself on an overdose of healthy exercise, a string so thin it could never make a knot let alone fill a sandwich. So we sat on the box and stared at the sea, all its situations folded away inside our hands. I no longer think there was a canvas in the box – it was Schrödinger's Cat. Look, the pier is on fire.

22. Glowing

Glowing red arrangement of paths with rocky trees by Friedrich. Tunnel through the forest and betray who it is necessary to betray. Carry a tray of offerings to the picnic table in the clearing: a chalice of bitter communion wine, well chewed, and an assortment of odd buttons, some of which are conkers, well chewed, and Little Red Riding Hood, well chewed, binding coming apart, pages hanging from the net on threads of stretched pink glue. The gods lack curiosity but nevertheless would love to see the coat that had conkers for buttons. Fake Irish passport in a fur coat.

Look, the pier is on fire is a basic surreal motif artificially inserted into materialist language. Burning piers as far as piers go are not that rare but in the big picture that includes horizons they are peculiarly memorable. We see one and ask *is that one of the piers that has burnt down*? At such times the sea is the culprit it is the sea that has burnt the pier down in an ekphrastic side-glance at the priapic gold.

Look, the iceberg is on fire. Now *this is* purity – the stain of the pure on an impure world. This stain is so beautiful the sea around the iceberg blushes then the sky around the iceberg blushes. The iceberg has an under-cliff where *souls* already melted into dirty water huddle dripping false memories of the fields and forests. In one place the under-cliff recedes hung-over into a cave of tarnished silver, its walls scored by ice-age graffiti. *This stag has spiritual quality* says the whimsical archaeologist that has taken up residence in the TV evangelist's glowing corpse.

Now for another snippet of story telling with supposition. Two men collect their wages and go straight to the nearest pub to dispose of *the greater part of it*. They sit in a cave-like corner of the bar *for the greater part* of the evening saying little yet each has a secret they've saved with which to impress the other. Once relaxed by John Smith's they release their dogs: Arson already a head in front of Larceny.

23. First

First Class. First class passenger. Second Class. Second class messenger. 3rd man theme follows second man's echo. City night. Second man follows up first man's steps in prime numbers then descends English as a second language tracing out the scattered themes of class. Stiff upper Middle School Moon partially eclipses a Catering College. Some things just don't catch on but I'm sure somebody will call someone will come to see the tall crane skate across frozen classroom discharge.

Flotsam. First class flotsam. Jetsam. Second class jetsam. This Jet/Flot equality is no excuse. Excuse me, is this seat taken? Excuse me but is that flotsam yours? Yes I know that's my jetsam I wasn't asking about that I was referring to the flotsam. It's not yours? Sorry to bother you I was just about to drift away not *drift off* as I'm expecting a call they charge enough as it is. Is this the queue for a seat on the Council or *Coastal Erosion Night School* or the *Grange Hill Theme Tune Tutorial*?

One year the school taught us French. One French Year. We were in Year 5 no not Year 51 don't be ridiculous Year 5. I taught French myself years later to another Year 5 no I didn't teach myself French but French poetry did instruct me on how to ridicule dead trees. Yes (laughs out loud) it might well've been Year 51 by then (laugh again) time was slack old lagging when the slag slipped in the classroom window. I remember the photos buried deep under the first page of the red top.

First off when do forests decide to be fields when footrests in China get coalfields in Wales to hunt them down in *the fields of France* is when. Carboniferous princes dress as smutty train drivers and ask them for a tip and I work underground too writing subversive literature only blind moles read. There are many routes from the underground tunnel up into the *Open Air Festival*. I *performed* there once. It was rubbish. You've seen those fields of litter left over, well that was all my stuff.

24. Swoon

Swoon wash soft glass scratch. Rust trophies fight for undeserved reserved space on shelf life. Runny moon is a reluctant witness to my runaway ear in the Britons Protection I laughed so much at Tom's lines I spilt my whiskey over a Welshman. Multitude of mirrors in a pocket tinkle scrape crackle and splinter a warm hand bleeding and *taking one for the team* already growing a new slick honey skin. The referee's whistle is as rusty as those hard-won cups. I hope it cuts his lips open.

A tub of ten tiny balls of red snot. What were the chances? Nevertheless here he is the UKIP poet standing in for the snot, impersonating a swollen tongue. That's pretty neumenal don't you think when I don't understand something it squats on my shoulder eating an ear only in the mirror does verbal toffee look too familiar. Quantum mechanics makes sense because it is obvious that the ridiculously tiny must be *really fucking strange* it would be a lot more surprising if it wasn't. No?

Sometimes there is a TV advert I could have had the idea for e.g. that three-piece one where sofas have replaced the seats on a big wheel. Couples are sat on them looking as pleased as punch to be on the bargain settees but I'd be scared stiff as the wheel is turning with no safety rails in front of the sitters. From the top of the arc the grave of Max Jacob looks like Jim Morrison lying dead in his last bathtub and I can do a good impression of Aleksandr saying *Who took the custard ones?*

Beggars are choosers of sorts. They have picked their spots, including those that are inaccessible to their fingers. I heard myself think it, it was not just words in an accessible order. This beggar is horizontal as he begs. Isn't that a bit too extreme? Couldn't he sit up? At least then we might see the mice chained around his neck, each dangle squealing treasonable despair! The little squealers. The little fates. And an *expert in his field* is passing the beggar on the way to his field of expertise.

25. Gentlemen

Gentlemen, we have a problem. All our women*folk* have run off to join the circus. Who will feed our children? Who will deputise for us? In the gypsy caravan there was little room for book shelves but just room enough for a little one big enough to hold about 7 books. Must now think of a title for one: *The Verso Book of Radical Tinkers*. Can't be arsed tinking of another except for *The Secret Life of Lay-bys*. In a little room at the back of the caravan a bonsai forest surrounded a bonsai road.

The Ravens of Caractacus where just passing by the Cars on Curaçao making the young Deputy too open to flattery the cause of his chronic insomnia but one day when heat was radiating off the pavement like a definition of art he was shot by Bob Marley's ghost therefore that night he slept soundly for the first time in ages and the flattery he had *taken unto himself* flew off him like another definition of art. Or *flew from him* perhaps. Off or from? One wing called Peter one called Paul.

Lord Baryon sat for his portrait I'd commissioned this portrait as a jacket image for my *A New Geography of Romanticism* (available in all rare book sellers). Lord Lepton had arranged himself around the periphery of Vigée Le Brun's studio but it was Rolf Harris who was doing the painting under Le Brun's watchful eye she'd felt sorry for his plight saying he could do with the work though he would have to return to his cell by nightfall, humming something about a stairway to Devon.

When the lock on a box of mistrusted secrets corrodes like a sheriff's badge and the ref's whistle then urban rust must mate with rustic necessity, dust dilating on the bed springs. Rusty was my best friend's dog and a good friend of my dog Boot who had her own key to the heart of our house. But Gentlemen I'm very pleased to tell you that our problems are now fully solved for our women have copulated with wild bears and have returned to us, rejuvenated and ready to feed the kids.

26. Supposing

Supposing. Just supposing. Suppose that arts admin actually Shakespeared itself and only then found reason for losing a phony war by posing as Government for all. One reason given I'd suppose is that authoritarianism is a separate issue for a stray wagon forced to hide in the forest with no wheelwright for 500 miles. No, maybe I'm not practical but that doesn't mean I'm impractical or *without further ado* – e.g. Jack Bruce's *Theme for an Imaginary Western* invited yeasty thematics.

Back in the day I wrote a long stringy lyric with smudgy turquoise ink called *For Pete Brown* I don't remember any of it but it was *sensational* and oozed the spirit of love hearts, sherbetty but literate. Some lines were jagged and nervous while others were cushions on garden furniture left out in all weathers to be soaked by the rain and dried by the sun. South Dorset Technical College melted around me, every friend an acidic dayglow cloud while I went on posing *for all I was worth*.

That's not true *to be honest* I just thought it would be fun to remove the *sup* from *supposing* to do myself a well-earned injustice I wasn't really posing just eking out what words might mean when multiplied by the impractical senses and was not the only *freak* doing this back then there were many in what was later called *the media* who were experimenting by not taking drugs in a similar way. Quoting from the future the period of status plurality didn't last for long *to be honest* the writing was on the wall for all tribal peoples so Syd Barrett's brain got scrambled but I would live to discover Richard Barrett and translate Nostradamus with him.

Once in the Art College taking a workshop on Discovered Meaning or something equally daft an old feller up front with two wives but no pen shouted *What about Shakespeare?* It brought back the smell of sherbet from Barratt's Sweet Factory which swept across the park in Wood Green and turned me into a closet naturist.

27. Who

Who is it who walks into the forest? He creeps even though you cannot see him creeping he crawls even though you cannot see him crawling. He is hidden. He is walking into the forest. Into. Is he in there yet? At what point can we say *he is right in there*? His stretched stride creeping and his upright crawling give clues. Follow the clues. The eyes alone cannot remove the barriers that obstruct them.

I have a postcard photo of a barricaded street in Paris taken around the time of the liberation given me by a pupil whose uncle or whoever had been *in the army*. This pupil was unruly but *good at art* – I still have a felt-tip drawing by him of a sinister human-robot hybrid and sometimes I wonder how far this figure could walk into a René Char line before stopping to frighten the birds who disappear when there is a vampire about. I got that from Dracula. For me it was the best bit in the book even better than when Mina gets all hot and disobeys Van Helsing's orders by opening a window and taking the sweetest breath she's ever tasted.

Even though what will happen is impossible we know exactly what will happen. It's like looking deep into a flask to see how much tea is left in there. Can you? Can you see? Then you tip it up, unsure whether to put your mouth or your eye beneath it. I've seen this happen on school outings. It's quite funny. A stand-up could use it if he thought that his audience hadn't heard it before judgement day.

My favourite robot is K9. No surprise there. Incredibly impractical though for a robot as much as a dog. I don't like Dr. Who these days though. I tried to explain why on Facebook. I don't like Sherlock either. I tried to explain why on Facebook. I did like the reflection of Amelia Pond in an alien invader's shiny armour *mind* I've heard that dads used to watch The Doctor because of Leela in her leopard skins but the hand needs an animal's eye to remove the barrier that obstructs it.

28. Revision

Revision. Knee-jerk. Moment of clarity. *Dumbfounded Monastery of Mindfulness*. Self-sufficiency nowadays means chopping trees to make a cookery book. I had a vision of the future when I was young and it was so off beam it could be a target for satire I thought we might be thrown back into the dark ages by the bomb but not by *true believers* we were going to storm the temples of capitalism and sack the palaces of foul religion but never dreamt of this change of menu. Isn't a new menu just the thing you would expect a precognitive dream to *pick up* and read?

Evasion. Here is a drawing of profit & loss transformed into words: *infinite image plunges up into pale pink fire water etc*. If placards are held up saying *We Are Not Afraid* doesn't that mean that we are afraid? Literary historians of the future will no longer terrorize our descendants with precise dates leaving self-belief room to swell into Betelgeuse. Buddhism is the only sixth sense I can stomach for long.

Invasion. Blake having a nap under an apple tree. If the appealing apple that fell for Newton was the appalling one Eve bit a chunk from was Einstein right to peel off a continuous skin in curling space-time? I think so yes and so do wasps it is only the theological mind that fuses its apples. We had two apple trees at my old house you couldn't confuse: one eaters one cookers one sweet one sour one red one green. Comparing their sizes was like saying *now if this ball was Betelgeuse...*

Deep into the wood (not a forest) the long lost long-distance walker (not the Lost Jockey of failed myth) comes upon the *Dumbfounded Monastery*. Its outbuildings are disguised as that garage in a Parisian back street that tied our exhaust pipe to the roof of our Mini Traveller. The old chapel is disguised as the complete works of Christopher Priest. The walker chats to himself disguised as Reverdy chatting to the monks who come upon the cold stone slabs in an invasion of revised texts.

29. Dog

A dog that looks like a lion cub is sniffing around the edge of a wood he has come across. He has come across from the city. He has crossed many furlongs of fields and wandered down *many a lane* to get where he is in life. He has been spotted by other animals. These spots are not yet full size but they will grow and meet up and when they do the dog will be able to tell the difference between his curiosity and his search for food. He disappears into another wood to be wood grain again.

A crestfallen wren knocks back a cider pressed from a mountain of small change. Drinking here is a ponderous affair, fail-safe but stubborn. Unseasonal pollen the size of raspberries floats by on huge computer screens smelling of Sports Direct. The wren grows in proportion but what monster has a mouth wide enough to eat such a fruit? Call in the butchers. The drupelets are fish roe and the butcher is a chippy out of time. Out of place too for there are no fish and chips in this Chippy just kebabs pies and pizza. Pinned to one wall is a panegyric to a prize cockerel.

Beware of shop signs. They may fall. I've recently seen this happen in both fiction and fact. The lion cub is sniffing around the outskirts of a seaside town this isn't suburbia this is a deserted dog-pound below a full golden moon. So beware this deserted dog beware this moon it will crack open like an errant head on a cider. Fruit ciders are *all the rage* but only because their marketing wasn't left to bards.

Now be honest be serious would you really like to see your poem up there with the *Illuminations* like a loincloth draped over a washing line? Let's push this. Do you really want to be *The Light of the World* carrying your lamp through a copse slipping on mud slapped by branches and wading through cans before emerging on the back path joining estate to estate with your lamp snuffed out turning this way and that with a crap sense of smell and a spiritual hunger far too modest?

30. Line

A line of symmetry runs through the plan for a final time being. Hard luck if you weren't listening little wildebeest the mirror image of fate is filling in your birth certificate with your death certificate details, the registrar's face serious enough to allow a sycophant's laughter to well up from the dry riverbed. We're waiting for the boss's word to also *fill you in* crayoning a flag's asterism to unfold fourteen stencilled star grains. Oh and call in at the candlestick makers on your way back.

Astigmatism of rain on three sandcastles calls in at the bakers. On your way call in at the butchers and get some duck eggs. Will he have any? How should I know just ask. Squirrel made of seven black holes repeats the pattern on a pincushion but the needles are long gone shot at light speed towards the eye of the deity. No, the lances shrink will never reach never impart the gift of partial blindness and his other eye is neither here nor anywhere. Beware of shop signs. They may fail.

Very long-lived children with fat imaginations leave home in their dead parents' rocket. A needle formation flies over the dinky forest far below where two pink twilight hares write kinky novels to each other as they listen to the cries of a lost butcher echo off the trees. His cries at first rather cranky and selfish now speak of raw slaughter house despair. Are you wondering how he found himself there, reader? He followed the trail of blood but he was tricked it was menstrual blood.

If I was a lost reader I would draw the line at finding the stranded butcher stood screaming like a rasher of bacon whose Pope was once a round faced little lad in a Breughel. See how the theme continues note how Attenborough has scrambled up a disintegrating cliff while Basil Fawlty gives the commentary yes in Africa the constellations jigger and fold. No matter who lost whom this is the womb where we *found our feet* but do we follow this trail to its conclusion or to its source?

31. Sporting

Sporting metaphor defeats the object. Realism takes you right up to the moment of death but no further. Money is *no object*. Fantasy takes you back to your birth but beyond that the past still slugs it out with syntax in a contest that will never reach round 3 though 300 bouts ended on the ropes giving Past a chance to pull the bell sit down spit blood and eyeball the opposite corner where the subject that got here by defeating the object is a googolplex of anti-particles made flesh.

Oh it takes me back. Christianity knew what it was on about all right, Talk Sport and greasepaint, a chimera to buy over the counter with pocket money no object. Just because something is logical doesn't mean it's true just because objections are experienced doesn't mean they're real. This for example isn't real. You enter the maze at the exit and follow your nose. I would love to live for eternity but not in this intestine. At the centre of the maze the Flat Earth Society are quarrelling.

It's all smoke and Miró's. A magician who swallowed you *passes* you in the street true you were on your way to the *Library of Alternative Histories* to change your books but he didn't know that. People *go overboard* making links to join stuff not connected as if their own nature wasn't mystical trickery – better than drowning in your own juices, no? No path is particularly inviting. Feeling obstinate? Follow a silkworm across its bridge of woven wires. Far below us the sea is covered in a raft fleet of rubber mats. Perched on a raft the Flat Earth Society are quarrying.

Just 'cause the rubber is figurative mockery it doesn't mean it's been confiscated. Teacher might be experimenting. Once curiosity is quenched he might be subtle and devious again I know this from my stint in artificial intelligence. Look down at the sea as it *boils*. Is that a desk I saw down there tumbling in the briny? OMG, a man in a tracksuit is sat at the desk. He is opening a drawer. He is rummaging.

32. Final

Final ascent on adulthood is too steep. Take a break. The city streets are a creep. The creep is not as misunderstood as the unforgivable monkey the scent of the unforgivable monkey is cynically sold as its soul yet monkeys don't have souls, we know, only scent. The creep has a soul though, a damned one. It doesn't know this, if so it would tread more carefully on the creaking boards between the city and the hills. Dropped flask of brandy slides down the glacier. Break's over then.

This linguistic process can unearth truth or truth of a kind. An unconscious is not the *seat of the truth* it's too wide unwieldy and unmapped but it's where the pilot sits. Truth is always found squashed in the narrowest band of frequency but this is where the pilot aims for speaking jargon through his headphones and keeping strictly to the code of *The Brotherhood of Creeps*. Far below him on the glacier he spots a blemish and a fleck but this does not confuse him. He follows procedure.

An inborn memory of horror unearthed children. Our gang watched the shadows of deformed worms and a Nazi helmet *playing* just inside the gate to Hell, a black arched tunnel in the opposite bank. A brambled drop falling to a base of rubbled concrete broken glass and sprouting tufts kept us at a safe distance. We shivered in the holy heat, first day of the summer holiday. Propped against the tunnel wall the *Gerry can* caught the fouled daylight. We would have to be brave. Leadership was called for. I led our little party back around to where I had seen some steps.

Science Fiction snuggles up closer to the certain than any literary novel. This is a paradox. The climbing party included a Sherpa on automatic pilot plus the boxer that Paul Simon sang about this was a different party to the party above which would eventually break up due to impatience and hermeneutical disagreements. There is also a third party, called amplification. The creep turns down the street.

33. Latent

Latent envy. The man is meant to be looking at drawings but is drawn elsewhere staring and staring at the photocopier which won't work or not for him anyhow it is not as if he really wanted to multiply things now it's a one-way conversation the copier saying there's a riot going on under the blanket, mountain building at speed, while Snow White sleeps with space junk then marries wisely, her bridal train a light year white waterfall cascading down *Mount Perpetual Apparition.*

Trees have paws. Some trees have paws. I saw a tree with a paw. The tree trunk's foot was a huge brown paw. Trees pause. Some pause longer than necessary e.g. I noticed a tree that paused with me when I read a notice I pinned to it advertising the next Language Club: *Arthur Rimbaud + Open Mike. Musicians welcome (unless,* that is, *they are called Tim or Francis).* Proofreading the poster I realise the venue is the new swimming pool the date coinciding with the opening ceremony. Panic flutters in the heart of the trees. I think they envy my important responsibilities.

It's a potent event. A portent with stretched rips and broken ribs. We've all slept in those. Tents let all sounds in out of the rain yet the imagination has a field day running out of poison ivy leaves to draw. *I'm home dear* says the sheep you never had the nerve to eat. Go back to the drawing board now and recreate that shabby teen park summer eve with bitches in a bush waiting for the birddog on his bike.

So the mind drifts to the high diving board and walks the plank the possibilities are endless but generally alight on the second nearest branch. *Brains do conserve energy* I heard on Radio 4, a lark was talking about creative processes poetry as processed food for thought. The possibilities are uncalled-for. Watch the single-minded accuracy of a bird as it alights on its twig of choice. When writers discuss writing *on air* the forest reddens with embarrassment for a city insanely jealous.

34. Cynic

A cynic surrounded by animals. The cynic surrounded by animals is in charge of all the keys. If there is break-in he will be the first questioned by a copper even more cynical than he is. A man can be many things a commuter a cuckoo clock a locksmith. Some smiths are Christian and articulate about the daftest stuff some women are Christian mothers and some are just mothers. I'd rather drown in the font than be a born-again Christian I'd like to stamp on Boris Johnson's face too.

Beautiful words were carved into beautiful rock on the beautiful moors beautiful water rushed past the beautiful rock with some beautiful words of its own which the rock words were unable to reply to or comment upon with confidence. Dumb struck by original grace struck dumb by original sin either way the first thing a new element needs is words unable to swallow solids it craves a loose language. If you care so much, animal experimenter, then why not experiment on yourself?

Some mums overfeed sons who feed computers come-hither sums and I'd rather be smothered at birth than grow up to be an apologist – carve that on your merry *Way* as inky clouds leak over a fat highland track dribbling in a disappearing act. The attempt to be articulate about the beautiful *before you* too often resembles a *Write a hard boiled short story about soft water* competition facilitated by an Arts Officer but restricted to any twelve-year-olds who can fart the twelve times table.

Animals in the zoo grew cynical, much like their keepers. These enamel animals made of wood found a molehill disturbed by Jarry's bicycle cruising out of school with wild and witty jelly girls next to an eloping couple stopping off at a Happy Eater kicking up a leaf pile fuss owing something to the demands of sophistry and practical joke signposts as we're on our way to Hades in a handcart loaded with capitalist junk taped over by Cardinal Newman's *Sermon to Athleticism*.

35. Turn

Turn down the sheet. The forest is as wide as the day is long. The watch on your wrist has gone asleep becoming a naked cyst with a white bracelet in the shade. Turn down this track. At some point time will turn up paper aeroplane points to pace across a stretch of forest floor goalmouth wide – mental pointillism apace. Forester's pacemaker leaves labels tied to udders on an upturned milking stool's prudish splash. Pale banana moon-shake. Midnight sun weighs less than a sheet.

The St. John Ambulance men toddle onto the pitch with their stretcher, youngster with a virgin moustache and an oldie puffing red. They think they're running fast but it looks a struggle. The clutch of players surrounding their fallen striker part to let John's men into the inner circle. The injury looks bad but is probably not as bad as it looks and surely that is not a bone poking its bulge through the sock, the Argyle green turned a dark battlefield red? *No, best not turn the sock down lads.*

Sleet goes down one neck but in response all emergency workers turn up their collars. Alice is on all fours peering down a rabbit hole doggy forelegs flat arse in the air a myopic performer reading her own erasure but our night nurse is home in bed REMless, a backing singer in backless dress taming teals and seals herded in by a dog balancing on two legs like a doctor who just *turns up*. Animals know the hole, how if you follow your nose you'll emerge beyond the perimeter fence.

The dog is like a doctor because he looks just like a doctor and can make you well enough to go out there and *perform*. He is a form of homeopathy and so we come to the homeopath's chiasmatic forest path entered where a dried-stone wall has lost an unreported civil war and fallen in. We all fall in we *line up in line*. From a watchtower a loudspeaker broadcasts the register but my name doesn't come up with the snowdrops. It don't matter. I'm a bit run-down. I'll wait for the bluebells.

36. Sat

I sat on the bench in town and began reading the space opera I had just bought. I was impatient to get started. In the park a man sat on a bench was reading a huge encyclopaedia I sat down beside him and told him that I liked Stephen King too I was mixing myself up with my Dad. The day was as warm as a hot mirror. I then watched a couple in school uniform disappear into the rhododendron bushes *like walking through a wall* and in futile tranquillity I pictured a burning stunt man.

The artist *pushed at the boundaries* he pushed them right around the world then realised he was being followed not by other artists but by the boundary he had dreamt of a world where everything was art one in which he could anonymously disappear from judge drudgery and be an arty nobody with no stake in the world where, hand in slippy hand, the pair of truants entered the bushes. The boy was from the boys' Grammar (green blazer) the girl was from the girls' (blue blazer). Even from the distance of my bench I could hear their speech bubbles popping.

Everything in this book has been copied from cooked books and those unworldly early editions of *A Sociology of Punk*. The very first printing press printed leaves. These were *verily* taken into the autumn wood and *strewn*. If you were an expert you could tell these leaves from the natural ones you can tell them stories 'n stuff from the oral tradition. And what is left of our hands after the leaves have fallen? – outstretched naked trees silhouetted against a tight band of white winter sky.

Even from the distance of a park bench I've bought millions of words in my time and rented a few back out. Words are the boundary between us and the world. In the middle of the rhododendrons there is a secret den. I followed my dog in there once and found empty Actimel pots and a burnt corpse. It's a big mistake to think that Language is communication. They're connected yes, I'll grant you that much.

37. Turn 2

Turn down this track. It's a good one and should be played loud but not everyone in the room *sees* it like that. Scan two jays cavorting high in long pines. The track enters a clearing in the forest which opens, step by step, into a view of the whole world. In the distance there are even taller pines. We know what works as we've been here before. Perspective lent by telegraph poles. Only lent mind you. *Mind you.* The poles are lofty. They lean. They lean against us. The world is *against u*s.

The indie band were photographed only once with the manager it is dark now on a suburban hillside of a city by the sea roads encircle the hill cutting terraces to climb past cul-de-sacs the band performed only once but repeated this feat over and over in their heads only one band member returned to check for messages and imagine erased tracks. Another night a gym burnt down. It was empty but it only needs to happen once. One mistake. A favour called in. A treaty honoured.

The rags erect. This is the way I stand for it. Crows aren't really that scared just reminded in a flash of being what they are whatever that is. This is how they see it – living cars push a dead van over the edge the insane gully is a deep grave so is there to be used. A neglected gully just leads back to the beginning of the track where a bridge small enough for a miniature railway crosses over into woodland chaos. Rags flap – no there is no breeze. Stand your ground. Whistle a meiotic air.

Run down the bridle path to silver water on legs you thought you'd lost to a dire dream in a Liverpool bar an old Squeeze song was playing when you entered but is not playing now. Men are looking up, necks slightly strained to watch a screen. Horses silently racing. Nobody appears to be speaking and yet the conversation is deafening the men all wear dark and dull suits, any odd colour here and there denoting a female presence. Test the water. Dip your poison toe into Rilke's owl.

38. Family

A family of crossword compilers live in a tunnel that spirals through the reverse side of a 3D jigsaw it is not uncomfortable. The unwound weave of the carpeted walls leads algebraically to the quixotic maze centre which itself is strung out in a series of quashed lights not light enough to read in but too bright to make love in so *boffins* make synaesthetic war by taking x-rays of next door's nightclub din before it can penetrate the tunnel wall and lift the spirits of the war-zone kids *in quite the wrong way*. Buffoons are never requested to tell the same story twice.

Imagine an office block. Make it yours. Imagine working in this office block. Who owns this office block no not your boss not him nobody lives there either except the night which only sleeps there actually during daylight hours the night walks the streets having a laugh with its mates around that bench near the park – near the park but not in the park around the bench but not on the bench. This *family* make the bench their out of focus group round-up table. Imagine a bit of trouble.

With a little bit of trouble *one* can work wonders. Yes some folk work wonders. Others just work. *No worries no trouble at all Sir*. The office block is built of huge sheets of draughtsman paper no wonder it is chilly in here the jokes are about as funny as the canteen food but without them the place would be a real drudge. If *one is* lucky enough to work near a window two of you see clouds in high spirits.

The wind whipped the sea into a frenzy. Back in the day wasn't there a Hitchcock called *Frenzy* with a red haired rapist red bricked terraces and a snatch of sky in the eyes of the woman being strangled and didn't he strangle her with his tie tied to her scarf with his mum's scarf – the mother's profiled eye in a window? *This is my best side* said the *widow* as if she was a row of fishermen's cottages *so take my best side quickly*. On film the wind whips the row of cottages into sepia froth.

39. Mammals

Mammals in suits are being introduced to multiple puns. A blank space for your *personal* message shakes hands in sympathy with a lama who is trying to shave a camel while drying his hands on her shaving bib so turn your haughty head back to the mirror where the blood flows freely from gouges and slashes, a right mess that'll take years to heal like face-value scars on long faced gangsters. Gypsies are celebrating something that looks profound but is in actual fact a shallow trick.

On a cold bright Sunday in the winter in the city a bombed-out church welcomes the dignitaries' suits with its usual lack of fuss. The wind carries a hymn across the road to the barber shop and fish shop but the tune is lost the words shatter against the closed shops' shutters. Just up the road a man waits. He is watching the cars. He is impatient to spot the first driverless car. He shouts. He lets us all know exactly what he is waiting for. Please note: what he wears was once a suit.

In the window of a charity shop a little boy's Batman suit hangs on the model of a little girl there is also some silver fabric ruckled to resemble metal rippling and ripping under extreme gravitational conditions. An innocent b&w photograph of the nearby cathedral is propped against a pile of football DVDs – I suddenly think of the aspirations of early socialism. The bombers have returned to Mars but the sky fills with flying cathedrals. Only the smokers come out of the pubs and watch.

Slammers waiting to *take to the stage* were practising in the car park striding up and down hyping themselves shouting their lines and avoiding eye contact with rivals. One performer appeared even more manic than the others a skinny young Kerouac clone gesticulating wildly and jumping around as if a firework had been thrown at his feet. I *caught his eye* and wished him good luck he smiled back *Oh thanks man. Good luck to you too. Hey I like your shit. You're the real thing man.*

40. Young

A young eel is lying on the sideboard. It is telling its captors a load of old rubbish. Severe punishments have to be invented for these traitorous eels and a truth will be extracted from this Elver which is what this young eel presumes to call itself even if it means a bureaucratic nightmare the following week. Ah the translator has just arrived. Send her in. Hope she's not squeamish. Then send Nurse. I know he was impressed earlier by Escher's skeleton walking down the up escalator.

Back in the day when Van sang *here comes the night* there was one species of bee with a tongue long enough to reach the nurse's station without getting out of bed bee's tail unfolds its story unravels having easy access to fiction isn't necessarily a democratic ideal bee wouldn't go as far as Plato though back in the day it went a lot further into the cave far enough to hear the rushing of water when without warning its fiery faggot refracted into wave-like vessels of substitute denotation.

It should have stopped at *far enough to hear the rush* then tacked back to the cave mouth. Stopping would give the right edge the suspended metaphysical stillness talent deserves. Too late now. No way back. Bee passes a young ghost its make-up box in the dark to apply a few attractive features to its cramped position. Back in the day the smallest concepts making up the Fortuneswell bus stop buzzed and fizzed too fast to make concrete sense to a scientist without his instruments.

A fresh tunnel is lying on the sideboard. The sacks of fuzzy mustard are sandbags hung inside wide trousers pulling us down to prevent us flying off from the 40's, in the short term anyway. In the long term into the 50's and so on this weighty drag actually aided our flight which is why we explode comically daydreaming in the small hours. I've no idea who *we* are by the way – one day I opened the Daily Mirror and there we were – a grubby football team of grinning atomic physicists.

41. Parachute

Parachute. Desert. Wheeze. Sneeze the desert into the parachute. SF book jacket illustrator is accused of being a plane spotter an I Spy book found in his suitcase along with a shadow twice his size. *This is no coincidence* say the prosecution but the defence demonstrate that a shadow made of cheap grey I Spy book paper can be folded more than 8 times. A paper plane is propelled from the direction of the jury box. A pair of silk knickers drifts *across* the dunes and drifts *like* the dunes.

Not exactly *like the dunes* let's just say both riffs conform to drifting through the dictionary to land on the definition of *drift*. They landed on a *shadow double his height* in Robert Harris's novel on Dreyfus. Colleagues in the pub had not heard of him that's Harris not Dreyfus. Slightly surprising. The quiz spinning around us was sonically invasive one quizzer folding his quiz sheet 9 times surprising for a gOD who believes in a racing *man* but then only helps him win 9 races out of 10.

An indigo abyss above the SF jacket illustration is a thrilling escape from the self-imprisonment of fantasy. Strange but I'd rather sky dive than ride up on a ski lift dangling over withered shrines to human road-kill spilled on the hard-shoulder – a frayed sheet painted in blood hangs from a bridge wishing *Happy Birthday to Colin from Rita*. On the edge of the school playing field the plastic blue and yellow Minions drink flask remained unmoved for three months. It moved me though.

A tremor moved through nude dunes shaking the caravan as I tried to read *Man in the High Castle* squashed next to the portly man in the Blackpool carriage who asked what I was reading. *Dominion* I replied by The Sisters of Mercy I liked from Leeds who sang about Mother Russia in black lipstick. We managed to squeeze in the fact neither of us could remember the title of Harris's Fatherland then drifted into reveries until a man getting off at Deansgate shouted back at us *Heil Hitler*.

42. Know

You know that ragged shadow that cuts into you, the letterbox with teeth and a doorbell with a rosy nipple in a crown of thorns, that's the fluid edge shared by play and practise. The tennis ball *literally* flew off the cricket bat into the long grass. Crickets sang. When not being Alice the little actress stood on the edge of the long grass looking straight ahead into the curled emptiness of spatial forever.

Soldiers balance on the kerb to search the scrub. They look camp they look right in to the tall tangle of weeds picking *too hard* taking in too much detail while the escaped prisoner escapes further into the distant blur. The film director screams *find the bastard he'll be hiding in one of the portaloos*. Film extras sit on the kerb waiting to be called up for the praying mantis scene. Marginalia know when their game is up happy enough not to be juvenilia left back at base camp accidently on purpose for tattoo ink to fade or infect while paper-thin Euclidian geometry rots.

The bandstand is made of ice and dust but the comet is made of comments made about poetic language here on Earth. The project was committed to going back in the burning house to collect a paradigm called *rocket science* but broadsheet arts commentary wouldn't allow it, its double-barrelled lauding of personality cults with moral aesthetics never letting up, that equation of external attainment with internal drive that nevertheless thinks it's fine to threaten us all with extinction.

On the comet animals huddle for a group photo in warm autumnal colours – long ago they planned to escape on a humanist adventure in a quest for a planet made only of language. The essence of this fizzed up in Victoria Park Portland 1968. If an intellectual novice is debating with philosophers all the *creatures of the field* prick up their ears at *first light* I go out in the *dim dusk* to join them on stage. A turquoise tangerine is hurled from the auditorium. It settles a very old argument.

43. Wind

Wind runs into the wood to catch up with its own secret. The wood traps both of them. Translucent hands unpeel invisible skin attuned diamonds tremble in sea horse trees while a million miles away a cricket ball is caught clean and *the men* cheer. The guards also cheer in magnanimous mockery as the dismissed batsman *for no reason* remembers writing an antic sonnet in an attic about a mountain in Mexico made of mislaid correspondences between railway companies. One day he will return to Blighty catch up with sleep and once again be a sister's brother.

When simplicity becomes boredom illusion sponsors war. The news is not good. The *call of the wild* exodermises consciousness only in the mind of the watcher. I really don't know what I'm *writing* about I forgot to glue in my partial so when I read a poem the falsies partially translated it into fairy talk. There was a handbag and an arm putting a long pale hand deep into the wind in search of keys – multi-tasking was taking place. Complex moment. Cleared out grotto becomes a garage.

The wind runs out of ~~the~~ wood escaping in tercets yes each escapee carries *on his person* three thieves as back in the Nissen guards discover optimistic horoscopes astrological charts and a clutch of smug innocents. The Commandant picks up a cricket bat and proceeds to dash out the brains of a steaming Marie Celeste mug.

Redbrick mill chimneys sway precariously above a back-street pub in the forest. Yeast evolves towards sentience having decided it was time to reread Rilke but couldn't find him as Amazon had replaced all his books with adverts for poolside furniture so it returned to the windy hotel room with the lido still whizzing and zinging between its ears to find J.G. Ballard sat on the bed spouting awful right-wing rubbish. Yeast wanted to unread him there and then and get the next flight home but its burnt-out suitcase was weighed down with a thousand pure malts.

44. Life

Life-size model of the new hospital includes on its sketchy perimeter model trees representing what's left of the surrounding wood once the hospital has slid back its doors. Pure maths is sullied by an alien appliance a smearing machine sliding large numbers into the miniscule causing dermatological damage to the model's face – bad news for a muse she may have to crawl back to work in the architect's office saying stuff at the photocopier like *Load it up* or *Occlude my itch please luv*.

If you follow a path at the back of the hospital you can get down to the rather un-dingly dell where a brook from the moor zigzags through an ancient forest of tall lolly sticks litter mud and corrugated iron. A rope swing dangles over a one-eyed waterfall where exposed pipes shirk work and shredded pools trickle to a damn of tat, the path ending in a dank tunnel beneath our improvised civilization's one-lane bridge. The swirled grey hospital cappuccino froth has an *afterlife* of its own.

Inside the head an ocean swirls. Its lava rivers heave its molten surface swelling. A Hokey Cokey chain of doctors and nurses winds through the wards in search of the manager where stillborn baby Jesus is taken from his cot to make way for the new arrival. Father Christmas is a blood-soaked consultant from my wheelchair I overhear him say to a Madonna in red shorts and dressing gown *pile the presents on the bed then load 'em on yer back. I can't scratch mine wearing these marigolds.*

I only like coppers in TV procedurals don't trust real ones any more than my first person singular once my friend and *I* were saved from abusive claws by the law and spent the night in the police cells of Wells we had been hitching into the dark prematurely singing Riders in the Storm when the blue knight picked us up. Not yet cognizant with Glastonbury or John Dee despite *the occultation of surrealism* we discussed The Yardbirds behind the cell door's locked or unlocked? mystery.

45. Restaurant

The restaurant under the sea is only there to make money its chief chef lives in the glove box of the owner's sunken car the glove box kept dry by their humour. Far from the sea but still under it in a whimsical sort of way three Dryads sit on a branch overhanging a pool making seven reflections of Dryads instead of money. Which for you is most real, the Dryads their watery doubles or their +one profit?

The explorer returns to his study. A Victorian meme. A fossilised flying machine sits in the theatre gods bored yet alert a thing possible in description but not in fact. The explorer turns to his wife and says *what the hell are we doing here when we already have a great great grandson whose restaurant under the sea is already raking it in?* Act 3: breath pours in as money pours out or the other way around who cares? Well, far from the restaurant but still within its toilets in a whimsical sort of way three carers clean up several theatrical pools of piss shit and vomit.

A street of terraced houses crosses the country. There is no way out of this street except through a house and out the back. All the houses are occupied so you have to knock and ask making contact with a thoroughly modern family knock knock. The door is opened by Little Boy Brush – *Mum there's a thoroughly modern man who wants to come through.* Mummy Brush shouts back from the kitchen *OK but make sure his moustache is clean.* You cross the threshold of a starved black hole.

The conference on Christopher Priest's Archipelago fiction concludes with a fish supper in the Waterfront Restaurant. Travelling salesmen find safety in numbers at their own table but overhear island-hoppers still talking shop: *This is how I get my ideas* says a brush salesman nodding at the literary jokers next-door picking at the bones. At his feet a wire-haired terrier has fallen asleep in his case of brush samples. Tomorrow conference will resume to discuss the fiction of Julien Gracq.

46. Head

In the head 1973 stately home and estate. A sweep of lawn down to a lake where a film crew fuss around Elton John's paddling grand and piano stool. The plan is for the star to play the entire Procol Harum songbook but as he hasn't turned up yet the crew turn into the fourth estate waiting around fidgeting with notebooks. The *guys* from the band in 1963 Beatles suits secretly hope it all goes wrong and going very wrong it is. The fountains are already refusing to flirt with the statues.

Plymouth 1974 the Buttery Bar on the basement floor of a department store is the setting of an LP *cover* showing the waitress looking over her shoulder at the *artist*. Her name is Shirley. She could be winking but just about isn't and could be smiling and just about is she has the air of an air hostess but this is her Saturday job. Also rendered by the early 70s album art are the seated clientele, red faced heavies stuffing faces with tea & toasties, fifty-year-old Gertrudes from the fifties.

Plymouth 1982 top deck of bus. Two girls in their early 20's talking about music and bands. One with disdainful disinterest is saying negative things about Queen then her friend replies with *Yea some boys still like that pompous stuff.* The future races towards them through the bus's front window already exhausted but they would never dream that it *Plymouth Heralded* an end to their post-punk republik. Sat behind them on my cloud 9 way to work I'm reading *The Good Soldier Švejk*.

In the head 2015 going through the Brush's front passage towards the kitchen you hear the granddaughters of Miss Stein in *Reception 2* hawking wares to any man who might *put his head in the door*. One man stumbles into this small press fair fumbling in his teacher's briefcase for a well thumbed *Out of Everywhere 3* full of domestic cliff-hangers and big wheels silhouetted against rust red sunsets. This isn't his town but fans have reserved him a plot in a corner of the cemetery.

47. Fire

Fire curtain falls on *Noye's Fludde* cutting off a child's tail while the wood turners return to labour in the backdrop, vain human humility intact. The Party's branch meeting blossoms in a run-down rural industrial park spread under a rookery. A note on van parked outside says *Warning: No words are left in this van overnight.*

If young Brush was a painter he would be a super realist whose photos look like pictures let us amuse ourselves by taking a snap – muse peeps through the bush and sees *that man* that's enough amusement for now agreed? In the middle of the wilderness there is a lake in the middle of an island in the middle of a cabin boy who's found himself a nice nook on the map of a fault in the wood turner's table. When the wood was cut down the Little Folk had nowhere to live so they burrow inside earphones can't you hear their tiny tin-mining drills in high-pitched block and tackle damage? If a hunter was a photograph he'd be abstractly brushing-up.

Shadows walk onto the dark stage, actors that fiddle with guitars and pedals. The lights come up in-sync with the music, turn to your partner and whisper *is this a kitchen sink drama*? The actors leave the stage in a darkness echoing with ghosts of literary feed-back until the house lights dissolve them then they can return to the stage as their *true selves* – humble human vanities bowing over washing-up.

The old hunter stalking his teen muse through the forest for four days + fourteen nights is yet to step upon her tail. He is now covering *old ground*, every underfoot crunch a long slow vowel. Having long forgotten all imperative judgments he can nevertheless sense their absence in the symphony of the trees, a forest of leaves shifting gently through the registers. Perhaps he should just stop then sniff the air like a hound but if he had a tail he would not wag it, poor soul. Is this what it is to be lost? But no sir he is not lost, he knows exactly where he is in the world.

48. Old

The old city is stood at the crossroads there's nothing to be seen except fields of stone and four grass roads – north to the transparent sun south to a neon moon east to the sea of mountains west to the Brechtian blues. The camera as political tool is useless here. Mother dances with spies Father climbs a burning staircase to the icebound stars. The devil is not in the detail it's found in the sprawl. Three erotic factories float in a harbour extended to the horizon. Poetry is screwed on.

The new city races past the twisted cross this bedsit is full of historians and their histrionic students failed architects and their thin paper languages corridors of stenographers whose wastepaper bins are buckets full of their aborted auteurs. In a glass oasis a popular novel being read by an unpopular guard kills what's left of the century arthritically curls into a abyss of self-referential pain then blooms into speculative beauty. If Jerry Cornelius wrote *texts* they would resemble the Robber Bride. An early Soft Machine gig – the future swallows its dystopian voice.

Meaty rumour computes two underfed WAAFs on a call-up poster hidden behind overgrown shrubbery. Poison drizzle. Favourite information. Revamped virginity in a virtual baby-boom choreographs the archive. The blitzed-out night bebops in capital letters slow-handclapping clocks that echo across the creased photograph of a flâneur's shadow. City splinter limebath block/figural rabid dead decoy duck.

A man is stood at the bar standing drinks for those not yet standing this man is crackling secret assets, burning radios, melting handcuffs. He waits for the poets to arrive back from the dead he is London School but this is a ventriloquists' city where predestination stutters in an endless karaoke smiling sardonically a form of jawbone jazz wodge war. The *bird* with Maigret's intelligence but too strong to take to the air is perched on a signpost draped with Magritte's hat and overcoat.

49. Luck

Luck gets absorbed into shoe laces the lacing loops city perimeters intersects and interlocks salad days with fast food nights no not sure if I like that. No I don't like that. Let's just call it a day it didn't even bother to say what was intersected but characters in novels are nowhere real enough or far too real they never have that indeterminate quality of characters encountered when reading *Life*. I had a good socialist friend who used expensive paper to print quality *avant-garde* quilts but I prefer medium quality paper that cuts shadows in two – into two sheets of light.

Shredded adventure threaded through the lindens matures as luck would have it. Barry slept with the polar bears who were sleeping too as luck would have it but in his dream were the bears eating his liver or drinking from his polished shoes? A professional has style even when on his knees he grazes with the cattle on the bitter black grass beneath a moon the colour of a tramps' plimsoll which is an invocation of sorts. Having the luck of the Irish doesn't have to entail being Irish.

Midnight on the frozen pond: Lilliputian lovers from the music box are practising a waltz. Mushroom likes going to poetry events because it makes her listen to the material unlike reading 'em on a page when she can't help thinking she could be reading a better example or relaxing with entertaining prose which unlike poetry is not conceptual – all of it is conceptual so-called conceptual poetry is a bit of a dropkicked moniker and certainly no antidote to the dictatorship of the elixirs.

Mushroom's dancing partner is *Minus This and Minus That*. Long after dawn has threatened to melt their love they are watched by horses who wonder if they are still, technically speaking, skating. The differences between shoelaces skates and hooves are quite important up to a point but as luck would have it we are well past that point. We can no more practise love than the starved can digest a feast.

50. Save

To save embellishments you must lose structure. You must enter that fair forest of resurrections acting as floridly as a carpenter's rejects. Celibacy flowers from sandbag torsos and shapeless vases, a tesserae tease. A Cornish rugby team have entered the trees too in search of the North but they are not *The* Cornish Rugby Team just their nemesis, absurd ambition. To each according to their meanings from each according to their savings. My intellectual appetite is a potted history.

It's a must-see history of asymmetry a vast sideshow of wise sayings that can be put up and pulled down like a circus of wise sayings such as *Is he who enters the river for ten seconds dryer than he who submerges himself for ten minutes*? but of course it's not that wise because the answer is *Yes* I've tried it, it was a must do experiment. And it's silly to say that science and art are similar. When teaching I got kids to choose a small area of the play-pound each then describe and record the daily changes but I got bored with it around the same time as the class did.

According to a radio report acting as if it was a reverse dictionary *some pockets of resistance remain in the North* though it is hard to credit so I lock myself away in the oval map room look out the rugby ball window and see an imposter from the rodeo standing bow-legged in my office block doorway eating my lunch. He is trying to read my post-structuralism book too but has no way of holding it while eating and there is not enough time for him to prioritise or even save up for later.

Now look and compare the seasonal changes on those who entered the forest for ten seconds with those who stayed in there for ten minutes. Ah just as I thought, fewer changes on the second group. Some sleeping in doorways have been dead for two weeks as well I stole that I rifled through their pockets and culturally appropriated their imaginations before the coppers turned up dressed as coffee cups and of course the homeless are dressed as take-away cartons holding dregs.

51. Work

This would work. Instead of secular hymns and followers at my funeral just show a series of clips from soap operas featuring farewell flowers and actors' tears. No worries concerning character let the dramas accumulate it would say something profoundly funny and I'd like that if I was there, a big *if* of course, an unfinished work of temptation dragging the Siamese Twin melded to my shoulder like an angel into existential dens and drug stews as mythical puppets clock-on to dance.

It makes you giddy where nobody works but it works fine. The young blackbirds in the garden are having a fine time too. Nostalgia scoured to its bone – thesaurus machine shop melancholy zipping up and down in busy boredom – Mrs. Gaskell's *North and South* copied out by Kenny Goldsmith for his homework on *Pulp Non Fiction*, it's a good read too. The paper mill on the right bank of *Ramshackle River* cropped up on the left in a dream where the canoe instructor was *a* Lyn Hejinian.

The pathos of the city's trees had something sly about it that was bizarrely both part of the human world and alien to it as if a logarithmic humour was working its way to the surface of the streets, a biodegradable astronomy of the soul or an hypnotic anagram showing how the shape of a forest is not the meaning of trees. Neither are analogies either, not for us, not for each other. Rain falls incessantly in the derelict factory. A cloned cauliflower and krooklok rendezvous on a slab.

If this was from Tattered by Magnets *Dig* would now appear followed by *Ballast* but it isn't. The semantic thought patterns are similar but the execution is far less jazzy more like a classical song in the form of a deferred Freudian fiction trying too hard to be reader friendly as it spasms and pulses, a ballet dancer making us dizzy while coolly smiling as if the blood in her head was ice, something no muse could do for language however talented, whatever her charge for booking tickets.

52. River

A river is a city state. The maxim *Empty vessels make the most noise* is from the same family of dodges. Vessels now have a rival in the container business, virgin automata blinking in exhausted starlight at *privates on parade* who snigger as a ventriloquist fart finds its oh so *soulful voice* in a flagpole thicket impenetrable to anything thicker. A city state discharges into *unacknowledged legislators*, not its canals, and while on the subject shouldn't the Laureate be hereditary, flushing into the river with its patron? Even mathematicians just have to add up sometimes.

The men had long hair. The women had long dresses. The lectures were too long. The lecturers were a mixed bunch. The college was a mansion full of the ghosts of German spies. I didn't hang around. One of the shoulder tags on my tatty combat jacket was hanging off sometimes a grey Saab that I really liked gave me a lift up the very long drive. It was a short drive. The most memorable day was when we sabotaged the local hunt it was the only time I felt one of the crowd. Sky cracked.

Keep saying *river* and the piece is bound to work. I know my stuff. If the original urban tag is indecipherable then the Country File translation must be an original too. The word *reverie* is longing to be used but so is the word *ire*. Bare branches break against the sky as the wood suddenly fills with one huge horse carrying an angry man in a red coat. The hate in his red eyes made me *see things differently*.

Hey it's all happening. Cricket is being played with Spanish guitars and matching statements. A drunk next to my drunken self said *I don't like soldiers or the police all soldiers should be arrested for what they're willing to do for the bastards and all busies shot for same reason* I nodded drunkenly but then he burst into song with *shirt lifters of the world unite* so I had to correct him saying *No no mate it's Shop fitters of the world* as we burst into a record shop basement with the latest flood.

53. Difficult

It's too difficult trying to draw an abstract expressionist architectural drawing of all the things money can't buy. If the messiah arrived by taxi it means he's holed up in some hotel so go back and check then get yourself down to forensics to put a boot up their lazy arses. OK Guv but the cult's worship of the triangle is difficult to argue with as triangles have a lot going for them which means that by turning 180° a lot is going for us it's as if the universe is always the new Argos catalogue.

The Echo Museum put *Sine wave* and *sinusoid* in separate display cases because although they are the same the former sounds scientific and the latter poetic. The tiny black-listed river entered the wood on the shiny back of a beetle to enrol for a compulsory course on novel writing. The beetle was a *simpleton* and difficult to understand but the river's voice was as clear as cufflinks. The sound of waves in a shell is an echo of Corbière's nauseous love affair with his own adolescent *hare*.

If I ever got around to writing my autobiographical novel about teaching it would be like shuffling off my wet pyjamas in the pool then diving to get the submerged brick which is what the kids used to do to get their swimming badge, well worth the choked spluttering wouldn't you say? The nuclear subs snugly throbbed only 400 yards away I say *yards* because this was the dockyard in the hard nosed cold-war 80s when the Navy was one suspended concept in an unfathomable dream.

Funny how it all comes together. If in Dove Cottage on the hunt for a first edition Kurt Schwitters then you'll come across five Japanese *adultescents* four of whom find it difficult to stand still while one is as calmly centred as a hairpiece chased into a lake by her idea of what a Wordsworth is. And it isn't easy to stand still in the sea either *mark my words* on Lake Galilee beach Jesus was trying to preach with smooth oscillation but had to compete with Beefheart and an ice-cream van.

54. In

In the 80s the stuff began writing itself regularly again after the 70's scraps and scrapes a textured Zen virus of white-noised Gothic squeezing octopus ink onto fresh mapping, contours be-bopped and borders cast, the linguistic electric of an insomniac's dreams. In 1982 I went to the League Cup Final between Spurs and Liverpool with two Labour Party racists when the car got to London I had to listen to their *torrent of hate*. Back then we had no black and brown in Plymouth.

In *Flamingo Valley High* the micro economies and Shakespearian dementia have to share the bathroom the school is famous for its diagnostic passion and drama lessons taken by handsome young Antonin Artaud. It is *a most unusual colouring book*, goldfish bowl heaven and deadpan disease. The whole point of theological bad breath is to encourage the phrases to big each other up utilising place value so any description is finer than what it describes in utero vertigo thimble sponge.

One of the racists was my mature student teacher badly overweight with bad feet so he wore plimsolls. I scraped him through the practise but his tutor failed him – the right balance. A mythological creature is one who always memorises ghastly images e.g. Pope Pius 12th said *we're just bits of meat floating around in the soup of survival* but as he was a turd floating around in a fascist gruel don't give it too much attention. Savvy platitude piety show vamoose. Evilly epic evangelical clog.

In vatic haste screeching liver birds surround the lily-white cockerel – we'll have to hurry to win this match before the game is lit up by an egoistical own goal. My goals are the best souped-up Tourette's you'll find this side of the Big Crunch *Oh Slobbery Dan Milosević O Tubular Bells O flickering fucking flood lights* each time I open the bathroom door I announce *two shillings and sixpence* using an authorial anus search engine to exchange an itchy optimism for this outrageous apparition.

55. Scuttled

The scuttled cradle lingered on like alchemy in the enlightenment. The sea bed it lingered on on glowed darkly like alchemy in the enlightenment. The cradle was a canary lantern on a humility spree a romantic state affair a factoid battleship in a salt cellar in a glass case made of sea-haze etc. I also *have in my possession* an old Chinese ladle dug from Yangtze silt a corroded dog feeder that spooned iron smoulder down the throat of a demon summoned up by *Li He & the Guard Dogs*.

The sea itself is a monster, a horror museum. I love the sea. You don't have to pay to enter this museum. The other day after microseconds of worry I had to wade in fully clothed because my dog was swimming after a ball too wide to grab each time she tried she bopped it with her nose so it just bobbed further out then just as I got waist deep my stubborn dog got her teeth around the ball and turned I was so relieved I didn't mind a molecule being a heavy drop of dripping sea soak.

My shoes will never dry out. When the Universe comes to its empty end my cold wet shoes will be the burning hot hole into a new cosmos. That's poetry, no? Isn't that what it's all about? – a sputtering and infectious hormonal information sheet of predicted text that guards the space separating the sacred sea horse from the profane NAAFI manager or the no-place in which the ghost of tooth ache and illicit pleasure can play safely without being called one or the other by any old scholar.

Belt and braces went to the races to bet on a horse The Oxford of Morse. Maurice the Ox the source of this childish evidence was seen lingering outside the courts pacing to-and-fro rehearsing vital data by shuffling Top Trumps – top stats for a sensuous makeover go to Cuttlefish blushing its asphyxiated trance bubbling out *What will be the breathtaking sentence?* and *Who will be on your dinner party list?* Well Kurt Vonnegut for starters and you Cuttlefish plus any primeval soup stars.

56. Detox

A detox regime enters its final days incandescently healthy and *to be honest* it's a bit sad. Intellectual entertainment comes with listening to the news on Radio 1 an unashamed overdramatic rupture of all mysteries finished off with a feel good fact. You can't beat it except with better music always found everywhere else. A routine rationality has spotlight jurisdiction and the scenery drags its feet onto a prayer mat. The *Red Skins* control the stage in a school production of Peter Pan.

The house was built for the high seas furniture screwed down etc. but remains becalmed in a branch of the civil service my mother worked for that lot a cold-war clerk helping to keep the nuclear tadpoles afloat or not as the case might be. Did you know the swirlies on Ken Kesey's bus were whirlied Portland dockyard paint and when the neutron bomb was dropped on Plymouth all the doors and fences slapped with Devonport dockyard paint vanished along with the people.

On a desert island you only narrowly miss your own culture yet miss the island's cultural references by a mile. Hanging fruits first detoxify then bring you down with Clubhouse Flu. The Pranksters spray locker-room talk on the Merry Men's lockers while Robin hugs Marion close inside a tree trunk, a stimulating sample of *Grand Design*, a secret room from a subterranean childhood. The last hours of the cruel regime are spent burning the bureaucracy in barrels and trying to cry.

What happened to the neutron bomb? Watching *Grease* ten times didn't help. An arrow in *The Prince of Thieves* also watched ten times (I'm a family man) only took out one Norman at a time but Jeff Nuttall was Friar Tuck in a lesser known Hood film of the same year (91). A bit weird all-in-all and whoever is holding the ladder please stop shaking with laughter and concentrate on looking up my skirt. We've got to repopulate the world by lunch time and honestly you're not helping.

57. Acute

An acute sense of future taboo won't save your tissue from an oblique encounter in the here-and-now. Looking as if lost in thought though actually lost in battle the whitewashed shadows of metaphysical art trek the length of barren beach galleries then back again in the time it takes the bay to cross half a universe. The night allows us to nostalgically creak like latticework and look cute in *unsuitable shoes* while a noxious *trump* asphyxiates us all behind a black-washed window.

I would like to thank everybody here today I would like to thank everyone toady too the list is long. We could be here all night. Any actual amphibians lurking in the gardens of this lush hotel would be contemptuous of us if they knew us but they don't so let's continue, I would like to thank you here tonight. Your support is love. Your help is evolving. First and fore. Last but not most. Finally folks – I could not have done it without those flies in my eyes and dung beetles up my ass.

The second wind is a bit off balance. Things that need saying once attacked by a bout of coyness tend to need commas to coax them down from their room. If it needs saying only once then as Mayakovsky said more than once *it must be as misunderstood as iron and steel* (something like that anyhow). When *the wind is in the easterly* as Mr. Jarndyce says it must be laden with a box of miscellaneous triggers knobby buttons swapped over levers and wicked switches of the West.

Mouse puts its head over the parapet. It is a pet without an acute sense of its own importance. Back in its master's pocket (Wilfred Owen's perhaps) it dreams of a world without masters even though in the current phlegm green mist all the misters appear to be doing their best to get rid of themselves which would leave masters with nothing to master except flamingo mistresses – decoy meditations trained to reduce importance without a loss of human value? Difficult to pull off on one leg.

58. Senseless

Senseless foliage can keep it up for ages but sensate fools can keep it up for ever. What the night remembers the day forgets. The body is a colonised vertigo plus a home for old yet underused bridges made of egrets so white the swans look dirty grey. From Southport looking west the stormy white horses make it appear as if the coast of Ireland had moved 100 miles closer in the night, white cliffs aglow in morning light or mile after mile of seaside hotels, an *Opposing Shore* of palatial vastness compressed too roughly, eroded by the book with the sandpaper jacket.

The Elementary Meanderings of the Trash Angel had a rough night rehashing old gin-soaked desert tsunamis Monroe krakens and dragon breakage necks mouldy with pinko honeycomb, avalanches of crystallised Pharaoh rolled in blue serge to spiral down the stem of the working man's orchid. In December 1966 a troop of W.H. Smith carol singers melted nighticehousehearts in a sacrificial mist clearing.

Multitudes of grey identities dance across the face. This face is a penal complex of dune rippling. Hecklers don't heckle but open up an alternative cave system from the neutral ear to the famished brain then refusing all options change everything back again. Beware the handful of hypersensitive smiles greased for speed full of ripe intent and ready to lend a feminist ear to the neutral intellect in return for a frosty definition of identical uniquenesses. The cake you must have and must eat.

Once you've mucked about with the obscurity of Copyright to make it a very rare bridge over senseless worlds no title change will irrigate folly like getting a bunk-up into a *state of grace*. About turn about time we are about to go on air when the latest news coming in alters what this sacred heart hologram was going to be all about. Earth – some facts. When animate we are a constituent of the troposphere, sluggish yet elaborate and asking if there's any point in still reading R.D. Laing.

59. Aardvark

Aardvark wasn't first on the ark he missed pole position 'cause he had to wait for his Mrs. who was hardwired to be late. They finally squeezed in after Sexist Beast but before *Simian the Uncontrollable*. The ship's manifest was written in ancient Haywire and the bills of laden all said Hay-on-Wye how do we know this? – smart archaeology of a surveillance camera's diversions swathes and levitation zooms kicking in a 3 ft. door ajar in the footy commentator's 2 ft. wide corridor is how.

The corridor is cyberpunk male but Kafkaesque only from the perspective of the trees. The rooms are one enormous hall through which the corridor runs like the mechanical wormwood of woodworm's vision. In the hall computable archangels waltz with computerised animals and they both find it 'ard work. Bet you're glad you came now, seeing through a birds eye the long corridor box splitting the hall floor of eternity into *a game of two halves*. Bet they won't believe this back home.

And *it comes to pass* they do not believe because it wasn't *captured* on film unlike the steam-punks the news caught sinking into Morecambe Bay. I'd dress up too if my Victorian personality wasn't sunk into a modern C21 cockle character saying *tidal décor be-blowed* isn't it preferable looking standard than feeling daft when caught on camera slithering in a Josef K mask down a long corridor towards trees where unhinged machine gunners have hidden a swinging fire door to the 60s?

Yawned deteriorate stiffs in the throat. Pushed cavity resists blandishment loop. Journalist pulls cross-channel swimming Goth out of headline and slays *natives* armed with an English dictionary's quicksand rude trifle noises salvaged from a bulging cast list of possible symptoms e.g. princess in tower block crying *Herne the Hunter be-blowed, I'd rather be a catalyst for the bloodiest ever contest for my honour*. And that's not Aardvark on the ark either, it's a copycat crime ant eater.

60. Placebo

Placebo gold diversion kept in proportion kept as daisy fresh and definitely spry as a first communion procession of asthmatic feather boas. Elsewhere always has an alibi in eccentric nonchalance always able to be itself *at the time in question*. A sky of incurable romance rises above expectation as a mean little breeze baffles a picnic minded mind the impression is less that of a crime and more like a sea of placebos, a dissolved system of jurisprudence bowing to a shrine of hailstones.

Plucky grieve communiqué skindle. Blurt daps reef impaction. Grafted strifle boo. Currently no. 2 in the queue. Tux comely bastard twins win an ugly smart phone cladding plus two bogie pal drogues. One country is bad enough but having over 200 is ridiculous a state grows its own placebos but this one is a fantasy empire and the other bloke's is genocide and slavery – *fear's your best friend soldier so keep him close – and without our guns buddy we wouldn't be free to follow orders.*

A wowie zowie Puck bores through solid moonlight to poison ears in the pueblo. The weirdest sights fashioned by nature are languages attempting to deal with a customary discovery e.g. what does it mean when a Native American is correct to be proud but a pale Pilgrim is not even one growing up ungrateful being fed on lies when one day the book he has been reading blind opens his eyes – a shocking speech of abrupt understanding still echoing from wall to wall in his empty soul.

If you don't know what to do with your old sentences send them to someone who can use them wisely. Be proud. In the *War of Rival Moonlights* prisoners received parcels from home containing contaminating silences in the form of mufflers and socks. This ill-assortment was much appreciated and hoarded until Christmas Day when the guards made a swap with a copy of *Tractatus Logico-Philosophicus*. Neither side believed in god but placed a lot of faith in their homeopathic Santas.

61. Chicken

The chicken house was an example of impeccable workmanship. The fossil vamp camped on Whitby cliff top wore an ammonite tank top. Close up the spirals spelt spells that only her boyfriend got close enough to read but never near enough to comprehend their impeccable mystic credentials. They had returned to the same camping spot to relive last year's déjà vu skills which they learnt running around the cliff top with stakes through their hearts and heads chopped off. Infinite fun.

It's all a metaphor for something. The timelessness of time perhaps bouncing off the mirror's language pretends to prove untrue by experimenting with imprecise memory and half-hearted predictions. If love simultaneously displays both least and most need of metaphor what does that say about the efficacy of the concept? The couple in their tent on the cliff top perceive each other's bodies as extensions of themselves while the skin of their temporary little house allows in alien lights.

A craftsman struts around inside his coop, trapped by his craftsmanship, cooped up in a sports car, open to the elements. The craftsman struts outside his coop. A strut has come loose. The Valkyries are hackneyed. A young witch carries a hen towards the chopper. Hell's Angels are not Gothic the way that angels' wings are feather and bone and sinew. Angels squawk. We saw a suburban squaw hitch a ride with Hopper on his chopper. We all saw it. We went to see it. It was noble.

Not being into horror films I'm going to make one called *Hickory Dickory Dock* to see if I enjoy it because I made it myself I do not intend to be *in* it it's not that I'm chicken it's just that I need to be in control of who screams and when and clearly why. The things usually offend my sense of black humour with their childish lack of disingenuousness fully faked as adult density being acted by offensive teenage Vikings with floppy fringes, but this one would be crafted to resemble an egg box.

62. Art

Art College portcullis comes down on cream horn. Cream horns are pastries that look like ice-cream cornets they're domineering top heavy defamatory baked in puffed-up Dalian pastry, a comic simulacrum of radical innuendo ruder than nine railway stations sat on top of one 'n other approximating that tableau of drunken girls in Piccadilly waiting for the last train home to the sober Styx. The happiness theorem impulsively gave an answer a bit too hastily for examination purposes.

At Thin Lizzy concert making a concerted effort not to be seen to be embarrassed by a head banger at my table. It was 1976 Lizzy were breezy and brazen the beer was stale insinuation the club boss announced next week's band The Sex Pistols I can remember never hearing of them the image in my head was the silvery black phallus of a seedy cowboy. Bomb sites in Plymouth, a stone's throw from the post war rebuild, survived into the 90s as wide open-air markets and chilly car parks.

There is an affinity between everything and nothing it cuts across out-of-bounds decks whether a pack of cards or Boaty McBoatface heading in to drop anchor in the *Bay of Approximates* off the coast of Proxima Centauri B. Standards must be raised. Raise the standard. Raise the Art College drawbridge before those skilled at drawing bridges and boats come raiding for the college could spill conceptual blood with sharp palette knives. In a parallel world Antarctica is playing tennis.

Maritime art auction. Phil Lynott was cool and handsome. If biological accuracy is your task stick to it and if engineering expertise sticks its oar in your shoulder blade on the assumption that it's an improvement don't quibble just think about the narwhal's tusk and the gorgeous nautilus in its marvellous house. Think of a quartz mountain thrusting through mist and a secret niche in a coral reef where the sweet artistry of a million budding polyps bloom into teeny Sid Vicious faces.

63. Extreme

Extreme ephemera reveal vagabond dexterity. Curiosity congeals into formality and brittle architecture, snapping into dust showers at every silly criticism. The Philosophers' Stone turns to soapy jelly which the apprentice slips into a pocket where it melts into that cream lolly I tried to save for later at Saturday morning pictures, a demeaning introduction to science that was rather more memorable than the Three Stooges. Not the meltdown the poor apprentice suffered though.

Extreme prostitution in the pot-hole of the night. The Maenads follow an avenue of knots in wood down a tollgate queue to a Titanic lounge where a poker game continues *as cool as cucumber* even as the table tilts in fact the cucumbers firm-up even as the warm water chambers freeze into wilting runnels of rot. But this is tepid water gambling the result of publicly-minded cowardice or plain-sailing tiredness not the heroic male's last stand against the madness of aging elements.

The gods are younger than the Earth, the recent results of dormant thunder and gaming. Most of them act stupid, on a par with a Terry Wogan or a Zoë Ball, but they live in such extremes of alternating poverty and luxury that excuses need to be made even if they remain simple anti-humanist gestures. Very useful extreme evenness in architecture and literature lengthens the fear waveband until even a reactor meltdown cannot fail but entertain with those domino effect hypotheses.

Meanwhile extreme storms turn the coral reef into a desolation of a trillion grey Sid Vicious faeces and successful cryogenic reanimation remains one of Sleeping Beauty's less obvious dreams on a par with trying to play Go against Snow White using a Seven Dwarves chess set while simultaneously avoiding eye contact with an 'andsome one-'anded Prince. Wicked! Note: this is a venomous sequel to last night's reverie, not current extreme topicality, a typical trait to try and replicate.

64. Archaeological

An archaeological lunch of the oldest whisky ever is helped down by a catapulted vulture poultice followed by more whisky and volleys then disturbing inroads of stillness and silence. This is utilitarian war. A lunula, fatally restricting, is found hanging over an inventory of bones and swallowed pebbles identified due to its interlocked hemispheres the remains of ancient continents sitting lumpen in the midst of juvenile violence. The brewer connives with the weather to distil frenzy.

But it's not all bad, utilitarian war at least gives the appearance of ending the rule of incessant nights of inane study giving adventurous types the chance of scaling the ivy camouflage on the facade of Limbo while a mass exhalation of held breath fills the fabric of freshly designed Olympic flags throwing rainbows in a challenge to the drained blue of the sky as if to say *I dare you to feign neutrality by hindsight with your stale gases loathsome sweet nothings and out of this world communism.*

In fact nothing is said. The digger of trenches knows there are missing factors in point of fact a war of words between scorched earth flagstones and an obediently busy factotum who just gets on with it whatever it is without complaint. He'll get a posthumous reward divorced from the fields and forces science has disclosed, or that's what he imagines. They didn't tell you did they that following battlefield death the corpses go on fighting not according to their country but to their class.

Now cometh the lesson, a personal remark to make it easier for the archaeologist to fill in a report. If however you have never embarked on anecdotal importance take care when choosing which mundane incident is to be the placeholder for the incendiary substance, or you won't convince the experienced reader of anything. Experienced readers know that a catapulted vulture egg is addled by experience. Abstractions may not crush you to death but you can still be seriously scrambled.

65. Initially

Initially the shape was infuriatingly precise yet unrecognisable standing askance in the Preston Vue foyer and must have been advertising some forthcoming art-film blockbuster. I didn't know if I liked it or not I didn't know what it made me think or feel apart from these limited speculations in other words the shape was a plaything shuttled between the objective straight line and the subjective curve – don't you just hate the avant-garde sometimes. The lack of simulated empathy is really scary they do the good stuff when their de-voicing devices glitch and glow.

Chase the keystones to a beach while delivering the speech with spittle for pity's sake as unexploded suppositories erupt from the collapsing scrum of Keystone Cops, a Zen den breeding sympathy with reality and what it has to endure but the beach is too hard on reality wearing it down to basics before we have a chance to hear a *thank you* in a keynote speech. It has too many cardinal points to follow with sense but no zenith and this is just the start too of what could be a very long weekend and that's not counting Sunday which initially we never signed-up for.

Any *thank you* grovels to the *guys* should be kept for the plenary but long after the projectionist has been escorted from the hall. I know etiquette when I see it I've even signed for it those crystal white furs I wear are home to a million fleas and innumerable more bushy little vagabonds and each one listens intently in a phantasmagorical fever to the prophecies being handed down from the stage by a man with sport in his eyes but signs of indulgent lassitude around his mouth.

What the creative impulse wanted initially was someone who'd give originality a good shot but I took this as calling for the deconstruction of originality whenever it appeared too natural. Hence this revolt's pathological reliance on shape, even if squashed in the Vue vestibule between the popcorn machine and a tank of Coke.

66. Sequence

The sequence of membranes seeks the open air. In the open they could be shot at because somebody somewhere will miss them. The Red Cross lorry delivers new batches of murder ballads to the jukebox. Hands up all those more interested in a world where they can't read and write than the one where they become a famous writer. The cinema auditorium crawled with flying bats so I spent the entire film desperately blinking sat with my arm around Joan of Arc while nursing a coffee that never seemed to cool then a migraine began eating away the corners of the screen the film becoming too subtle, a subliminal promotion of sly quintessence.

The relative respect given British POWs by the guards was in stark contrast to how they treated the Russians and Poles they gifted Russians arable land where enormous diamonds could be turned over like potatoes and presented the Poles with pictures of the Immaculate Conception which transfixed and imbued them with misty eyed spiritual terror, something to experience in a teenage graveyard.

The opposite of subtle is explicit. The Portland quarry boomed, followed quickly by the disembodied screams of the angry film director. We have met him before obsessed with gore in a dismembered forest and debauchery in the buried stars. He's got countless awards to his name but it's not a name I know I never know the names of *these people*. The quiz master exchanges value with a slave master.

Excavation of the Milky Way began in the heart valves of the early humans in the cavernous clarity of carnivorous night far away from the coniferous forest where only the conifers could talk. By the time the saints were walking on the Earth our weather had gone through a sequence of unheard of hyperboles. When you walk into a wood you know the trees can sense your presence. Hum a tune because a tune has no lies, only possible errors, beyond any uncanny detection by the trees.

67. Kiln

The kiln was communal. Whoever or whatever, nobody owned knowing it. There it was not mundanely mysterious no not at all of it at once. To use it at least once you once had to put your name in a book and if you did not know what some of your name was you could *go through a friend* and if you had no friends you could go through a barricade of old clay pots to emerge the other side of the jail wall. In this dream prison a student wanders repeatedly around the cusp of a passé fail.

Excavation of the kiln began in the library. The library belonged in earnest to all of us. In the outside world the books earned differing amounts but here in the library of democratic poisons having no time for books gave them all equal space on the shelves. A lot of equality has an aristocratic feel – just imagine a nest built with ears cut off Conservative candidates. Happiness and tramlines. Birds and outskirts. Through the open kiln door you glimpse a forest path into the library.

If you are searching for symbolic relevance you won't find it in this room. Indeed the kiln is very much like a room but if it was a room it wouldn't be this one. The room is like the underside of a flat Earth but not this Earth if this Earth were flat. To use the room you must erase your name from the book as if you were sitting on top of a mountain wondering how you got there and now how to get down it's enough to *get you down*. Once down please feel free to *ask questions of the Media*.

And while we're on the subject are you linked in or lifted in or do you work in the sand factory suffering cramps from the damp lifting a little Englander weighing as much as a big British bloke into a balsawood glider launched from an aircraft carrier using a huge elastic band or are you a dust magnet microwave sat on the kiln in a cupboard strangling a water bottle that has already been throttled by a graphene stalk twisted and knotted into a bucket and spade made of graphemes?

68. Small

Small world looks out at the expanse of space as it slopes away slopes off tilted like a tomb in a *depression* but hey the border of the universe isn't out there it's probably inside us. Precocious starfish hand jive contagiously, unhampered by health concerns. Poison spray is smuggled onto the astral plane then released at an opportune signal from *a member of the public*. The rebus machine switched to max drops slurring bombs. A vote is taken. The dead float better than the living.

Yes it's depressing in fact it's all so bloody awful don't look anywhere too closely every second white man is a third black woman and the soldier boys sent on film to be disembowelled on the Normandy beaches make a postmodern fascist the President of Gilead. When this fed-up put on The Fall sit on the radiator play with the dog have a coffee or if it's summer go in the garden and share a frozen yogurt with the beautiful sex objects called bees while annotating Frankenstein's jotter.

Having no idea how being small has made what I am untrue I revoke the right of the delicately balanced giant to know that when he falls in the forest no sound will be detected by psychic researchers for the liminal alone is the improvement on heaven that purgatory represents for those who don't just *see the bright side* but live it to the max, the rebus contraption sacrificed in a shoddy Faustian pact in order that no-one has to care for the fate of poison frogs or divine orang-utans.

The annotations in Frankenstein's jotter are stylised gut feelings but no longer a personally felt cliché. The smallest hunch grows up too soon and leaves home but can easily mistake Bokononism for Pataphysics which is why neither should be practised by retired revolutionaries wearing fabled *kids gloves*. Small wonder the *Ch Ch Changes* were not what Ziggy was thinking of – the romanticism of Berlin sharing the same Vera Lynn as the rest of us. Go on, roll me over the cliffs of Dover.

69. If

If young when starting a masterpiece and old when finishing it then gladiators pitting strength and cunning against immovable objects in the pit become middle class butchers devoted to a form of golf from which sport has been extracted and all status transferred to the social – 'twas always on the cards yet sports science is sprouting up in every college green. These contradictions, the stuff of history and fairy tale, are the blind twins abandoned in the touchy-feely forest of the burglar.

Literate slaves of illiterate religion are trying to decipher the motto on the fridge door in the dark with the burglar's torch. This is an internal messaging service, a drop-in point from an alternative universe delivering an equation worked out by an amateur or at least someone not paid for their atheism, hence the temptations of crime. When challenged by the householder immobilise them with a prepared quote while the rest of us escape out of the cat-flap with tails between our teeth.

Embalmer's flimsy finish unravels the iffy history of the forgone conclusion, the universe of the falsely accused. Criminal law is a statement of fact put through a computerised creative writing programme for if a liar is too honest for their own good does this mean that Surrealism has survived its appropriation by fashion in *time* itself or just in time to be back in fashion? Anything that still has to employ its own name to be identified is a failure in imagination. Facts are useless faces.

I don't really like this literary incest. A huge gull flew through the house across the street but *on reflection* it wasn't in that room but flying outside mine. If this isn't incest it's nepotism, no, narcissism then, no, ok, the eighth type of ambiguity maybe. If you view the doubly reflected bird as an omen, an external reply to an inner puzzle, then you are not my type of twitcher even though, rarely refracted stranger, you wish to interpret this as autobiography falling into a random star.

70. Mountain

From the mountain top the lake almost has the same shape as it does on the map. From the lake in the *top of the morning* you can just see the top of the mountain climbing to the top of the morning's inverted reflection but the mountain's mass is hidden behind layers of amended mapping including draft sketches of a PTSD life study, a Marine not that concerned with the study of marine life. He pretends not to be proud of mental scars, another romantic bully in the crowded gift shop.

Fervently undulating inbuilt fault emitted a high-pitched tetrahedron that could outsmart any safety officer's report. I was one once and I patrolled the school on the pretext of having some idea of what hazards might be lurking beneath the surface of things. On the other side of the road a heavy water lake pretended not to be proud of its powers and threats. When I first went to Drake in 1975 it had a store of iodine tablets to be dished out to the kids in the event of a blow or a leak.

From there one could go on to greater things e.g. mental breakdown and cancer. A good job claustrophobia isn't contagious otherwise anyone lost at sea would be found later washed up in a reservoir's gift shop as a bi-pedal candle holding frog. This top-shelf night-shift walk to work in a procession reminds me of the miners returning after the defeated strike with heads held high. Each holds a candle and another frog's hand. The surrounding night is a valley, an incision in a *black sun*.

I thought I walked with head held high too but a beggar shouted *Hey po face, got any change?* – *Yes thank you* I replied *but not for you you rude bugger*. I only said bugger because of its likeness to beggar so forged on head down further into the bright black city centre. People were tripping over the legs of beggars emanating from every doorway. Yes *emanating*, an oozing form of effort at miasmic contact sport. These are the proud chimerical miracles of our very endangered species.

71. Sea

The sea. The town. The sea. The hill. The dyke and the swamp. The sea fixed. The sea fluidly fixated. The town bored of its people. The people bored of their town. The fluid on the knee of a lady of the town. The Doctor who fixes the fluid on the knee of the lady of the town. The confabulated hill. The sky coffins. The fabulous children. The poor. The children of the poor. The Sea. The town. The influence of the town. The influence of the sea. The dedication. The magic show. The eddies.

The pink swim in the repository. The relatively rich relatives. *The Dawn Treader*. The lugubrious experiment. The influenced rats. The happy few. The influenced stats. The crenellated happiness that describes what it feels like to play chess on a crenellated cheese-board with the guilty survivors, one after the other, of the ship that went down in the bay. You force 'em to play. You are the storm in continuing human form. Their guilt becalms you. Guilt is an ice-floe. The town's sweetheart.

The border of the observable town is an untrodden sea. Untraded goods float in a futurist animation whose pace and vivacity is projected with sluggish ennui by a machine from the *dark ages*. Yes, the speed of the sea is a shiver. The brightness of the town is cornered. In an eternal evening velvet reservists saunter along the promenade measuring hopes and wishes by whistling into the wind and waiting for the echo. Others just stay at home, preferring to be delayed by an idle fetish.

Over hedges over bridges over ledges over fishes. Far out on the remote frontier forgotten conscripts barter Acker's *Empire of the Senseless* for the Mekons' sung version. This is not a price it is a scandal popping-up anywhere because within a reduced literati stories travel faster than a messenger's guilt turned into theatre. The town has a little theatre by the sea with a car park that scampers downhill from the town hall cellar which is full of tortoiseshell lyres and untradeable gods.

72. Prose

The prose poem is a mindless form, the perfect vehicle for someone supporting democracy as a mobile festival of the freely flawed so it's a shame that one thing leads to another. Wouldn't it be great if, as I said to Socrates once when we both taught in the same school, democracy was more closely related to social context? We were driving back from an NUT meeting his Fabianism incompatible with my anarcho-syndicalism yet we never crashed we kept the debate buoyant. Plus he never swallowed the poison the kids gave him since he was actually Rupert Bear.

In a glade in the forest a ruddy yet rudderless sailor with a squeezebox sits on a log playing a shanty with sad words and a saucy merry tune. In a further glade a man-made Chinese mandarin sits on a natural stool gazing with automata eyes at some focal point, an abstract space, a mathematical construction. In the centre of the wood a tump rises up from the forest crowned with a ruined castle. Rupert and chums have come to a halt at its threshold, dwarfed by the socialist realism.

Bed crumbs will never be redundant, these tiny condemned to die conglomerates of realism are the seeds of our castles in the air. When our chums get imprisoned in one of these elevated dungeons the brave will keep silent for fear of telling the truth but the flying high will keep silent for fear of lying, spurting out that their rave days are not long gone, not if you are comparing scars with original wounds.

And here comes Ubu. Ubu knows the difference between a forest and a wood but he doesn't know the difference between a Polish wood of polished wood and the wig worn by the Pig King of America. Perhaps he is that king dipped in rosewater then spread too evenly like every *Papa*. But pigs are lovable and a Picasso sketch of Apollinaire makes him look like Père Ubu, face Googled in Council House pink and a big butt done mint green but neither needs the benefit of disambiguation.

73. Man

The man never thought of getting this far and maybe he hasn't for the scenery is identical to the late afternoon of his departure for the city. The same stars wheel in the sky and the same fern forest stands under a far too familiar gibbous moon. By daylight this forest is a deciduous wood sat beneath the sun and the city is not his destination but the home he left with a crust of gingerbread and a thin ginger moustache. The man thought he had entered a woman but she had entered him.

Last night I was left in charge of the bargain winter hat counter. My situation was perspicuous yet insecure. I'm sure it was me I felt like me but I looked otherwise and immersed in such warmness coming from the press of customers found this new job to the liking of my new self. But I was soon overwhelmed. They were not hats they were headwear and the difference was an essential one I was meant to have internalised. Then I was in the crowd at Hillsborough and couldn't breathe.

Adamantine superstition of man time. An emotional incantation accompanies the procession circuiting Victoria Park from red dusk to ice blue dawn. A fibreglass Paracelsus and silver Beach Boys head the cortège carrying the sandstone corpse of Sappho on a 24-carat surfboard. Following are all the blacked-up extras from King Kong and Tarzan but dotted here and there among them are my friends and seven diamond splinters ablaze with loving tenderness, all dancing in their sleep.

Heraldic knots and gnarled heat shields dog-fight over the *treacherous waters* of the Portland Race. Any loser here will not be *later to win*, not as an independent living entity anyway whatever the final score of the wider conflict. Further out to sea the sea becomes the ocean and further out still it becomes the fabled Library of Alexandria, the largest unmanned collection of science fiction in the universe where writers too clever for their own good lay on an alter to be slightly altered.

74. Isle

The Isle of Portland is not an island it's a diminished seventh chord or would be if it knew what that was. Its mother wanted it to learn piano but they were poor and anyway it didn't sound cool. The cool thing was a more relevant reason than the poor thing because they weren't really poor they were just normal, well not that normal either otherwise she would not have wanted it to learn piano. One part of Portland actually said a silent *yes* but years later could not even admit it.

The Island was a playground of corrugated iron. Its own children had great fun in the limestone jungle made of sleep-walking stratagems and gang warfare snared in tumbleweed and tar. This myth isn't a finished article it's just the first issue of a hobby magazine interrupted by the Gestapo's early morning knock on the door. That's not the real Gestapo it's just the way dreamers dress in a hurry to get that lorry to carry them to the abyss saying *at least now we won't have to walk there.*

Isthmuses would rather control their own torments. Real Gestapo wouldn't look as familiar as these *rum chaps*. As the real Gestapo are *German* so real islands are *Scottish*. An infernal brass band plays techno through a dampened bagpipe hum, the marching roads lined with snow and the worried synthesised smiles of those we have conquered. No man is an islander now. *Get over it.* This is the victory of the young Celtic nations over the Aryan sciences and Anglo-American olden folk.

But the road to the isles skids mid air. As there are no playmates for the children to play with in these parts it is fortunate there are few children in these parts let alone any with piano parts. Children have to play with the empty *strands* in their heads and fall in love with their cousins. The sea itself is an island. Its mother is a tin of blue paint mixed with sleeping pills and identical trips to town. Waves are working reproductions of one great wave that is sweeping us away as we speak.

75. One

One nuke sub among many newborn insomniacs hitches to the moors to drink in the essence of a meteor shower and bathe in its corroded gifts. What will become of us? Year's end is a drowned in living-quarters time reliving blanks in the diary blind spots the size of dwarves' beards cartoon bubbles stencilled exclamation symbols exploding hash-tags and punctured full stops. One *what* swims with the whims ends up back in dry-dock scrubbed raw by a crew of Tom Waits golems.

A skin-full of nanny of the Mary Poppins variety is twisted into a rubbery replica of a live swollen-up form by a children's entertainer with bloody weird balloons. Surely these inflated sections are specialist preparations not your run-of-the-mill liberal party paraphernalia being clapped and whooped by guardians awe-struck with parental incredulity even more artificially pumped up than the swell nanny.

Oh yes, the unconscious is folding in upon itself, Freudian puns regrouping for a last assault on the hard-hatted cordon of bullies and bulked-up cops. Veal crying on the lorry *Oh poor us, the water runs right through us*. Scalding crocodile tears spring from a perennial problem: after saying what you want to say any attempt at further explanation entails contradicting or calling the original statement into question. There is no alternative. If one swallow does not a summer make then neither will two half-hearted swims followed by three hundred days sunbathing.

There is something wrong with that shooting star though, the way it disappeared into the trees was askew. It looked too much like a man, a man who might think a tree thinks *how many of us are there* while the forest thinks *how long have I got?* If the city is on the lookout for a country girl to join a suicide pact why is she not on the meteor that has just made a hole in the forest large enough to hold a city? All the search party will find is one alien tadpole trapped in one muddy puddle.

76. We

We are not looking at the universe because we are the universe. What we see out there is our brains, an amphitheatre turned inside-out. The ebb of tapestries and grafted clefts of analogue that bestow and steal our daily loaf are themselves the bored lifeguards overlooking an ocean of trembling webs. A writer may imagine a dirigible star with intense convincibility but it is the scientist who leaps with animals into empty bins then laughs at themselves later on *You've Been Framed*.

Seaweed. A necklace of lamps adorn the Bay of Healthy Presumption. *Zoooology*. Trailing fronds of backward glances. The thieves are rich the crystals mediocre. The City Mayor is a woodsman on fire with political passion. By morning he is an ash pile in the clearing still cold with due the door he could have escaped from opening and closing with the tide. Love sucks then love blows – the breath of the midnight zoo. Geological rays pass right through musical shrines. *Poeeeetics*.

When young you are not too alarmed by what appears to be too easy. The alarm is a tickle in the form of an artistic tease. Sleep is discontinuous but the dream is uninterrupted. When no longer young *in the eyes of the world* you are no longer haunted by suspicion you know the harm everyone is capable of both bestowing and surviving – the arrival of a new face in your dream just a matter of statistics. Whether this pleases or depresses is down to what you gave the birds for supper.

What birds eat for supper is not what you think you gave them. Their midnight feast is what the dinosaurs left after failing to return from a crisis meeting where an addendum suggested that an inevitable loss of power could actually bring an incremental increase in possibilities. This is why nothing ever written down can convincingly follow the already written – any narrative wave of drifting attention can only be deflected by the desire to build an aviary much larger than the sky.

77. Crossing

Crossing the street to evade *a drifting invention* while tenderly watching columns of caterpillars sequence dancing a slow-weave between traffic pretending to be immobile. The lights will change to green, they will, definitely. Catch up the lanky legged Lorca translator then overtake him on a blind bend. But what if the lights change to blue? Butterfly would understand, surely, be familiar with that point in the evening when the forest turns blue in a forbidden likeness of unique stillness.

Everything is forbidden, that's the secret. That's why everything is funny even if the joke is only appreciated fully on sleepless recall. Every poem's a joke of sorts a ridiculous costume of language ephemeral yet strangely exclusive put on for a laugh yet endlessly adaptable to the mutual envy of shy lovers. Or at least that's the story that I hear so if it is true that context is everything and therefore illegal how come the similar has the potential to surprise just as much as the different?

Those who have been imprisoned unjustly or for politics or in a war revisit the cells escorted by a film crew. This never happens with those who were there for *crimes*. Only the guilty feel entirely innocent so would never return to the site of that darkness yet a criminal on release will have the same quirky dream he had inside without unnecessary puzzling over its inadvertent return while a prisoner of conscience struggles to recreate the unique groove dreamt while incarcerated.

The linguistic root for *motive* and *motif* comes with its own novel poisons. Cross the field to speak to the archaeologist without tripping over a city and win a ride on a self-drive tractor held together like a mud hut running away with itself into a corrugated iron shambles, all that's left of the prison camp where crazy trees go walkabout to avoid the spiel of the multi-discipline artist given a grant to *cut 'em up* before cutting 'em down. It is only sated curiosity that decides what's sublime.

78. Never

I've never liked my name. Never ever liked it yet never seen the need to change it either as that would imply an arrogance even less like me than my name. As I got older I liked the name less and less especially when I had to share it with that carpenter comedian who played Father Christmas. It's mildly embarrassing but a smidgen of silly shame is no reason for such a move. In the lagoon of impersonal sensations the pattern of ripples expresses what admen baptize as inexpressible.

I've never been one to moan about the given but admit to myself to having been slightly held back by my name. It was ok for a teacher but a bit bland for an avant activist or post-surrealist. *Tim* on its own is alright and so is *Allen* but together they suggest a loosely downhearted fixation. Nobody would knowingly refuse to ripple, would they? The luminous creatures, intrepid masochists to a *woman*, are trapped in the lagoon system by their own game of *Let's Name the Constellations*.

Tim is far too obvious a name for someone small and yes this is by such a clichéd parcel of acids. Maybe it was part of the reason for absconding from the school of infinitesimal grading to join the travelling circus of ambiguous entertainments in which animals are allowed to eat spectators in an illogical positivist orgy learnt autodidactically working in a garage where the pumps are *manned* by a mermaid in dirty overalls worn deliberately to contrast with iridescent albino Celtic skin.

The Godparents were a pair of seals buckled to railings outside an alehouse on a hill, Oliver Ahern and Teresa Coakly on the never-never of an expanding universe pushing the verses of Tim Buckley's *Song to the Siren* out in front of the different versions whose following progress is hindered by cat fights and sad anguish. In particular the sirens Elizabeth Frazer and Sinéad O'Connor enfold excrescences of mica and feldspar. Unable to choose between the voices I'm inevitably reborn.

79. After

After falling off the bike it's best to start writing another one straight away even if it is only the distance between the car-turning circle and the final judgement. A cocktail cruelly become you, verbally invades and looks the better for it. If you're so afraid of using a single word as an afterthought the barman won't be so you'll find yourself saying it anyway. It will definitely dissolve your image as a kitchen-sink beauty. This already sounds too normal typical of the drama school version of reality infesting the forest. Learn an index by using your hips. Unlearn balance.

The sea was a fugitive register flattened at the well used margins. Disaster dream tidal waves whistled behind as I swam uphill in search of our council flat yes you might well ask why I was swimming when the flood was still the dream's future, just trust me, I'm an expert on this stuff. Early annihilation was expected anyway and even now I sometimes think we are the ghosts of a world concluded in 1962. Next day though the sea was still there, a sea always dissimilar, always the same.

There is nothing original in saying that, that thing about the sea, but not all such observations are clichés even this one which could be applied to every new day and every object hovering within it. If this is where the sea becomes a metaphor does it imply the dissolving of the sea as matter, the sea becoming watery again?

There's poetry in the New Testament too, Jesus' seamless nightshirt. Brill! And feeling like a schoolboy he makes his way down a dry summer lane towards a hedged-in cottage where Mary Magdalene waits as if she were the sea following him towards herself like a creeping cliff of ice. A Dalí still-life implies time melts, or the instruments measuring its beats do, but to stop and dismount a bike you control imbalance, pretty close to the reversing of time. *A good essay* said the teacher *should look like an elixir, taste like a cocktail but choke you like a linctus.*

80. Quasi

Quasi monotony opens an era of astrological excellence where every prediction *comes to pass*. This level of skill eventually foretells its own decline into an era of untold error. Those Victorian military jackets looked great on Jimi and Eric the day I bought Allsorts in Petticoat Lane I saw those uniforms on racks and on the shoulders of young men already younger than me. Ah well. In the space between market stalls stood a woman roughly half Cleopatra and half Rosa Luxemburg.

Tension mediated. An example would be one of those mirror-silvered balloons in the shape of a four-cornered cushion ascending to a cheese party in Heaven. The guests sit around on such cushions talking in a pitch only dogs hear, though there are no dogs in Heaven their cheese is here on Earth guarding Rosa's grave from suited Dragons too proud of their ignorance *by half*. Beneath us the road surface changes with every step but with transformations too smooth not to be an advert for something – yet we'll never know what this mediation is actually promoting.

Low tide in the estuary. A shoreline of greasy stones not yet pebbled. Think rust and salty flotsam under a grey mid-morning sky but with the reds and yellows of the children's anoraks as brilliant touchstones for memory. Among the driftwood one of the class picks up the carved cat that still props up Žižek on my book shelf. The cat looks blind, a proudly frowning Egyptian goddess sat as erect as the mast of the ship that carried the bored sailor who whittled this horrid piece of jetsam.

Lush monotony preoccupies the lost Magi. Anyone know the names of their three horses? Wiki doesn't say just says they'd *a large retinue*. The slaves know exactly where they are though as years ago this was home from home from home so the air is queasy with spoiler alerts, yet no one speaks. Even iconographies of ethical forestalling fail to keep fresh Lacanian coincidences from impulsively flowering.

81. Quasi 2

Quasi meditation rips community hall into civil war. Dancers are taught division techniques by an Aussie backpacker who says he's sure he once crossed a river in Saudi Arabia. He has a female form too which he hands out to passers-by as if it were a leaflet she's a devil of a better dancer than he is and writes e-books of erotic historical fiction. It's too much. He can't handle it. This jealousy prevents him from going home for a holiday, as if someone he loved had joined the police.

I loved the feel of the plates of dry mud that had to be levered off football boots a week after the last game. They'd cling around the studs veined with grass blades their disintegration on removal into irregular crumbling clods made fingers feel reptilian, disappointment tempered by sensual revisionism. My first pair of boots were positively rustic, two misshapen buckets with tongues hanging like rusted shoe horns and laces as long as the distance between the penalty spot and goalie.

What's your point then? What are you trying to say? Nothing. Just as meditation is the attempt to escape language by chasing it out of the body and then chasing the body out of the mind so this is the attempt to reclaim language by dragging it back in, a photosynthesis of sorts, so as I said, *nothing*. The attempt itself is quasi literature, a cul-de-sac, a functional trap for the *spirit*. Alternatively escape with your housing plans up a ginnel, a pressure valve between front-parlour therapies.

And do not mistake those running eloquently on the spot for dancers they're just adventurers chased out of success stories back into the prison gym. If you cannot build a shelter then die craving other reasons and if you don't hunt then die from eating too many obese berries. If you cannot fight for a mate then lose the will to live. Horses dragged to the trenches to drag out the dead were hypocognizant in their silence they knew what was going on a lot better than the troops ever did.

82. Forest

The forest that once covered England is a source of intellectual energy. Make it sound meaningful. Enrich the inner life of the bourgeoisie. Dispose of your crap in the back lane of social history while seeing to be seen elsewhere giving your friends the benefit of your hard-won experience in anecdotal doses of disguised desperation while doubling back to some chromosomal quarantine. The tracks in the forest are rail tracks leading to a College to learn how to make silent films again to an accompaniment of cynical proverbs concerning the *archaic* seasons.

The forest is a failure, not a noble one either, but the confident way it whooshes past the platform should make us pause even more in our relative stillness, poke our thoughts with a walking stick to release what thought thinks of as ants from the hum-drum of their nest then scratch our heads just as automatically as any ant before noticing that the forest is still streaking and smearing. The situation is perpendicularly horizontal not horizontally perpendicular like a Keith Moon roll.

The role of the forest in a woodland is that of a drummer boy in an army of Girl Guides. The role of a room in a passage is that of Andromeda in a time and place so particular nothing can touch it. Wander out of the ward. Stumble upon a rest room full of rocks. The mine ceiling has caved in yet the boxiness of the room is intact. Scrabble up the incline of this obsolete TV mountain of junk to peer over the top with the head of a turtle but then hear the shell crack open on your back.

The old television tube found in the woods behind the houses reminded me of a space probe crashed on a comet – a horn calling out pathetically to its master. It was saying something like *pity me for I'm a little animal myself all lost and alone at the mercy of an unknown form of death*. I nearly said count yourself lucky son, many would swop places just to feel that their own failures were so specialised.

83. Shadow

Shadow circumscribes the loins of things as well as beings. Cremation ash cast by a loyal retainer on the passing of his contract spins into a ball of darkness, one no bigger than the world, then skims upon a glazed ocean towards outcrops and crevices. A ship of evolutionary wood disembarks in pursuit of the ash ball then speeds up to show how it all works. From the shadows of a narrow quayside ally a man now watches the deserted jetty. This man is a highly experienced widow.

Shadow that man hoping that true to form he'll return to the scene of his crime. What was his crime? Nobody knows or cares but this makes his capture all the more pressing, his eventual punishment all the more severe. When images need reinforcing this *handy man* simply pops up wearing his widow's weeds. Long ago he made a down payment, his signature a forefinger's hiccup on the tiny screen proffered by the delivery man. It is a hypothetical trace, a graph's sudden spike.

Bats' wings. *The Dumbfounded Monastery*. A thief's talons. The stapled shadows. Nails. Nail gun. Ben Gunn. A Davy Crockett hat skittering across the cabin floor to escape *the music of its peers*. Fleas on the hat fly between stations. Biomorphic conduct nugget whiplashes borders ambiguous accumulating staple cornucopic investments to bridge the loan of the gun. The monks burry the gun in the sand then return to the quotidian a little flushed, prayers blistering on their salty lips.

1969. In a church in Dorchester so non-conformist it must have long ago reduced gOD to the dust on the floor The Crazy World of Arthur Brown are practising new material, experimenting with freaky electronic screams and so on. They have a large dark dog with them who howls non-stop through every number. There are not many numbers. Some 25 years later I mention this to Arthur Brown but he cannot remember any of it and I think how can anybody not remember that dog?

84. Digging

They've been digging the tunnel for so long that the war has ended but another is now well under way. They bicker like a couple though this couple comprise two diggers two mules and a look-out who can't see a thing. The soil excavated from this pipe has disappeared from this universe but the stones have built up in the spare room back home where they picture a baby booming into the future. It's a shame the child is not theirs. For a while the schools were full of an unintentional anticipation, a full to overflowing reservoir of hope. Now their aim is *evacuation*.

A forger is asked if he can do clouds. Two clouds are needed, one stamped with a watermark depicting Attila the Hun and one inhabited with an MRSA munching plastic. The latter should look like Marilyn Monroe cuddling a poodle if possible but if not then it's not a deal breaker. The forger says yes though he has no idea how to go about it *It will come to me* he thinks *I just have to be patient and not panic.* The tunnellers come across a cache of turtle eggs. Fear paralyses optimism.

And then there was the anarchism of Murray Bookchin until it got all puritanical. Dig out an old pamphlet that still gives practicality a look-in with no reactionary backwoods stuff yet to sanctimoniously choke the seditious kids with sawdust. A trans lad in scraperboard make-up and pencil skirt impressed me the other day in Leeds but when I told him this he looked very suspicious I suppose he wanted something more drastic and durable. *Nobody told me there'd be days like these –*

Most peculiar Mama. Returning from city to city Saddleworth Moor tells me I am old it says I have nothing to say and that my history is not unique while insisting it looks nothing like Dartmoor but fails to add this is because it swells sideways pushing us off the road into the *Encyclopaedia of Cornish Saints* pushing between two other big reads: *The Interpretation of Arcades* and *The School Dream Project.*

85. Now

Now we come to a river but there is a bridge so *no worries Sir*. The bridge has a tollbooth so we hand in our forged ticket book we have come prepared we are not Hansel and Gretel we cross the walkway occasionally stopping to jump off into the void before renewing our relaxed pace. The wind carries shards of glass that skim past our faces we can imagine being cut to pieces before reaching the other side where a foreign flag billows sinisterly above an unmanned checkpoint.

Far below the river is the Earth, over-familiar and terrified of sudden silences. A rack of faded postcards hangs outside the deserted guard post this is where the ambush squads swop films so just as Bonnie and Clyde drive up to the tollbooth to be beaten and done away with so Sonny Corleone gets riddled with bullets on a Louisiana dust road. The streets of Dudley are dark and cold. I take refuge for the night in a local hostelry but around one-thirty I'm joined in bed by Queequeg.

Let's see if you notice what's wrong with the above paragraph. I noticed it pretty quickly but am keeping it in because it's a fine example of how easy it is to get a geometric detail wrong when rushing into the bigger picture. I realize that there are a number of things there you might think I'm referring to but no I don't mean them, they're quite normal. Hansel and Gretel walk out of the woods alive but are not prepared to tell anyone. Gretel says there are already too many stories to tell.

Now we come to another river, much smaller but without a bridge. Hansel says it is not allegorical it's just a river but a voice in his head intones *One wrong move and you get it, Buster.* The wind has died down. Everything has died down except the river. Within minutes the river is *in flood*. Within minutes of that it becomes too dark to see Hansel standing there staring at time, too dark to see that Gretel is now cursive, writing her own roadway to loop and swing through the treetops.

86. Come

Come prompt. The supplicant has to be prompted. Take umbrage. Take Umbrage back home, this film will not be good for her nerves. Be expected. All this lauded experimentation relies a lot more on subject matter and opinion than the stuff it is supposed to be superior to. The aim of the loquacious multiplicity and complex forms seems to be a way of saying that what is being really said is too important to be said. Arrive at the conference tired and late, sticky in unfashionable fabrics.

Sluiced hogs abandon a threshold to its splinted torpor. The tin mine perpetually incomplete hurls night breezes downstream. Spawn learn to spell but not how to pronounce. A tenebrous tango by moonlight stops and starts in muffled clicks. The air is alive drunk on atoms of the dead so how come a colossal condom is pulled over a soda fountain, a perfect fit, a prompt sheet troubled by the exact status of anti-matter? No, it must be a transparent standing stone, a code book torn open by the impatience of love. However that is heated human love, a Mare Clausum.

At coffee break overhear ephemera being slandered one delegate's chat comes across like the weightless somersaults those astronauts never tire impressing us with, another projects himself on the wall behind the coffee girls in a wash of red landscape. A woman, sticking to you with water tension, presents a practice pool you can tepidly splash in before diving back into the conference hall *but none of them are on the line or know what any of it is worth* so smugly hang around a bit.

Come look. The prisoners have eaten right through the gate. These tiny monsters all originally from the same collective farm now gladly disperse to the four cell corners of the world, growing like water and flowing like grass. Yet each actually seeks the same interchange, the gateway for translated scales where the frozen forest tracks meet the warm drafts that soar sideways from the glass-blown city.

87. Young 2

A young philosopher on a springboard doesn't question the vest and shorts this gymnastic club insist he wears after all the insistence is never mentioned and particularly not by the insisters however for the older philosopher long fallen back to Earth in what looked like a controlled flight, even if in reality it was less graceful than a wonky swan, that kit takes on substance. Still of limited weight and not vastly important but nonetheless notable enough to scribble notes about.

Pioneer photography in both senses snaps the Cherokee Chief against a painted backdrop of how the whites of our eyes imagine his wilderness in the iris. I'd say the arrangement was a genuine response unlike writing's deception begging to be caught in the act of returning eagle eggs to their eerie. How rapidly the vast is boxed. How slowly an ego inflates its mammoth prison. Certeau: *Tout récit est un récit de voyage, une pratique de l'espace*. Said with some certainty it must be said.

A bewildering multiplicity of bars. A complex of bars. Recto – bar. Verso – bar. Up – bars. Under – I think it's more bars. Yet when we colonized this bench earlier to eat lunch the bars were a distance off down the other end of the quay. I leave the bar and return as a stevedore to the quay, now verdant with moss, to collect my coat and wallet. Not here. I must have left them in all the bars when distracted by a sunray in the chilly canal lock while having to balance between perilous sills?

Mind your French in front of the young. Quoting Certeau once more with *Là où la carte découpe, le récit traverse* reminds me of an Eluard poem about being in love with a woman in a dream who he does not love in daily life. They are sat in a café when this loved/unloved woman, seeing him smile at a pretty barmaid, playfully nudges *Go on Paul, you're half way in there* or the French to that affect. Breaking open a crate of philosophy books I search for the poem in a volume by a *A Anthony*.

88. Sea 2

The sea has a history it has had nothing to do with. If geometry is really a part of orienteering then the lad failing 11+ was better at architecture than his teachers. The syllabus had many rooms but not enough room for revolving a restaurant. It is only by taking the floors apart then reforming them as a timeline that a hiatus of cause can free-up the integration of effects into wry reflections more attuned to the demands of the present occupants. Currently the sea is a very famous loris.

Whelks. Come on in. The class are having a geography lesson. Your timing is good as earlier it was maths and you would have been out of your depth like a ship on a *shipless ocean* already briefed on lyricism by the illuminated absences from the hierarchies of abstraction. As a dream is a day at night so a sea is an inventory of absences – gypsy children hiding behind baskets of poisoned fish. At this point a whelk would really love to raise a hand to interrupt this whimsical rot but as it has no hand it remains well mannered and lets the tidal speech wash over it.

Pandemic gossip buck stops at the butler's jumper he wears alone in his room when he wants to hate any histories of the Dead Sea but that's all there is to do so the threadbare jumper colludes because it's a war veteran spasm that wrinkles a scroll around a rumour creasing the winter garden faces of the other staff. Scenes from the war are knitted into the jumper trapping all tittle-tattle in their tangles.

This is how maritime navigation works: ask *who invented the first beach?* All are welcome to reply including the girl with the eyes of a loris whose name is Alice and has had next to nothing to do with her own history of seasick opportunism, a bilious loneliness designed to be experienced on dry land, a bargain future on the cheap oversleep. Overslept heroes here on Omaha are no longer amphibious they only answer to Fata Morgana beckoning them from inside a steamed-up compass.

89. Now 2

By now you should recognize the methodology the question is whether this has a detrimental affect on enjoyment. As the aim of the method is joy it would be a shame if this windfall from the tree of knowledge soured your experience. One idea is for a celebrity to pretend they prepared these poisons then see how many copies sold before revealing the truth. The profits could be shared with any other rich celebrity, only fair, hoping it maximized our capacity for politically free fun.

The day before school starts again a bargain geometry set still in its transparent wallet is left on the beach. Everything transparent in it, ruler, set square etc. has questions to ask of the solid compass but to be honest the whole pack left there intact appears to ask even more questions, of beach, of time, of the sea, of human stupidity, of the necessity of school etc. The Marxist sat on the sea wall dangling his legs and letting the wind turn his pages has hidden a revolver inside a *system*.

A revolver strapped inside the cistern is now a staple of thrillers and spy fiction and so too are female detective inspectors giving male detective sergeants good dressing-downs in men's toilets and men upbraiding their female colleagues in women's toilets a scriptwriter's meme calling into question habitual notions of higher education. No surprise then when a pistol is blu-tacked behind a pipe by a crash-proof girlfriend who has also stapled a Derringer to her callipered thigh.

By now the nature of things has ceased being mysterious, mystery having seeped into explanations leaving things themselves lonely unnatural and bloody minded, insistently heavy in their visual weightlessness. The mandate given by the combo spontaneity to forest city room and river has run *a* coarse and all have handed in their equipment. In our instrument zoo the Phoenix has completed its sequence without undue concern for the keepers as everyone is promoted with a pay-cut.

90. Cabinet

The cabinet was a psychic organism containing secrets that could only be opened by shock. Craftspeople need to sleep. A craftsperson performs miracles even very familiar ones that drain energy. There are of course occupations far superior to craftsperson: musician, business leader, journalist, policeman, celebrity type one, actor, lyricist, chemist, fraudster, sovereign, soldier, banker, spy, novelist, list compiler of positive discrimination lists, lecturer, middle-man, charity wallah etc.

There is a cellar in the cabinet which hosts live music events at least four times a week. It attracts capacities. One night weekly it is hired by the grafters who dug it out for the crafters it becomes an echo chamber reduced to words the creativity sounds remote and has problems making friends a sad state to be in for sure but one buzzing. The dead man would not have discovered the cabinet if he had not discharged himself from *Casualty* first and then wandered Holby's hobo streets.

A psychologist is a craftsperson, so is a goose. The most despised profession is a toss between teaching and surgery. Reasons for the former are complicated but fairly straightforward for the latter they are arrogant jealous over sensitive and bad losers. Television has a lot to answer for. I took a cabinet Granddad made to the *Antiques Road Show* and while cabinet and I both stood in the endless queue in the rain I shrunk while the cabinet swelled out of all proportion to its worth.

Who can afford to get old shrink and bend over? I have no crafts because I don't count putting the bins out and football. The closest I come to being anything is a sociologist but one that makes good use of geology and cosmology I can feel my head swelling now. When I hear formations of geese fly over I call out to myself to go out and have a look. If it's raining I try to look out of the window but that is a poor substitute as are the riches of day after day compared to telepathic shock.

91. Certificate

The certificate of insurance covers death from woodworm plus exhaustion from writing out so many certificates on Sports Day. It's a refined example of cognitive dissonance in action, days spent exercising your inner Action Man by adjusting a consonant cog then careering into Dodge with 107 substitutes for the relay team who've been practicing bumper car surveillance and rescue. The investigator is searching for a back-story in the taiga, one lacking artful intelligence yet useful.

You'd hope there was such a thing as an ethical music but there isn't. The Fascist father beams back at his baby's sunny smile and if he doesn't beam at a different baby that's not so unusual. Others have tackled this issue before when in the field only to find themselves queuing to have their books signed by the *Fascist Father* sat at a desk in the goalmouth signing copies of his *This Won't Buy You Out Of The Green Army, Mate*. Rightist romancers use cheery tropes similar to Pablo Neruda.

The fairground has no safety certificate. Music made in the hellish heaven plays itself out in heavenly hell. Balancing on the back of the bumper car is an electric Hyperion Tree sparking and unshaven. Leaning over you *he* steers the machine around the widest orbit then hops off to hitch back onto the zigzagging car being driven into the sun by screaming girls. He has already shed seeds in its footwell, an acorn bouncing off the walls of the very first thing we are impelled to imagine.

Back when the fairground covered the planet it had to fizzle out somewhere so it chose the vat of used cooking oil at the back of the chip shop. A postman wanders those streets still trying to find *107 Green Room Lane* it was only supposed to be a Christmas job hefting sacks of holographic totems but felt more like canvassing for votes while covering his multi tracks with narrative toxin, not a stubborn life-long vocation in a diaphanous cavern lost in the knot of a twisted accordion. Etc.

92. Horse

The horse receives its instructions: remove the human from your back toss the bugger in the mud where he belongs let the Hussar's filaments plume off tell him insects have stripped him of his rank. Run horse back to the field you were born in. Polite horse. The saddle slides away you jump the mad house and wheel away towards blazing serenity. A writer is always too ready to impart tough love – the last thing language is is a code but the last thing that it is is what it ends up being.

Horse tells us we need to make arrangements for when there are no more horses by pointing out that The Crazy Choir's nutty performance made horse 'n us too happy for our own good but that if we bought the CD it would irritate so what is the use persevering with making jam if you prefer your strawberries straight off the stalk? Horse says just because one of the choristers was blind it doesn't mean the rest were tone deaf. Fair point horse, after all we're all stone deaf *to a degree.*

But what does Seahorse say? Seahorse is supernaturally suspicious of all religion questioning whether any of its entertainment value is worth risking some pretty daft truths for for from the word go we've all been betrothed atheists otherwise gospel would never have gotten so powerful nor nutty singers required to think that way because they've been given divine rights to improvise. Knowledge is the equine arabesque of all turbot engines, a ghost music race, an also-ran candidate.

Discontinuation continues to be the surface marker of non-human love laughter and longing. Trotting beside horse the pointer's job is sniffing out fresh proverbs and isobars on the footbridge from the hotel pool to above all the shoe shop. In this romantic *western* Corrugated Wind gets stood up by Potato Flower and the cowboy on a horse dreams of whores while the cowboy asleep under *a blanket of stars* dreams of his horse. Horse sleeps stood up. Locked knees overlapping duty.

93. Attempt

It's the attempt at thinking of nothing that gives me nightmares. One phrase that describes it is *icy metaphysical terror* coursing down the spine to the base of the gut (autonomic system toads take note.) We think of *nothing* as a lack in a space called a universe so what the hell could a nothing be outside of that space? This is the reverse of my childhood bus stop epiphany – that pure question *what is stuff made of?* that ecstatically gave no answer but did imply at least two directions.

Place lacks direction. The border between Salford and Manchester concentrates into one specific place, a common trait of borders. A walk to work wakes you for the 4th dimension ahead then walking home loosens the gases even if the evening has its own job description. It's not just students of futurology who think about a city that can think for us. City is trying now. You can sense it in the small-talk of those who have not taken pills or been to the gym. Place doesn't care but is more aware than it looks, knows 4 dimensions are the ones it has to share with others.

In the rooms of *Everyday Life* guides similar to those in NT houses are available. Do not attempt to take them home you will only feel debilitating disappointment. Once removed the guides are indecipherable, especially the living ones. And take note, the rooms of *Everyday* are not those in your house just as the flowers in the park are only yours to sniff. Home is a veritable museum of hope filled hobbies.

When rivers of magma meandered down pre-nubile landscapes there was no one around to complain about valid cultural distinctiveness tipping over into rancid nationalistic idiocy? Pungent culinary politics attempts to waft the winners past the losers and there's a temptation to gloat back with that ethical superiority of the victim, but if you've read Nietzsche you'll avoid this and try something else. None of us know what that would be though. Even praxis is a little lava tributary.

94. So

So, the moon is ferreting around in the junkyard. So, the ferret is moonlighting in the wood the other side of the windmill so the windmill silhouetted in moonlight remains a pretty picture even if most of it is black and grey. So, everyone says *so*. So, *so* is the latest verbal quirk. So, I've looked this *so* thing up it's being used as an *interactional agenda*. So, that's that sewn up. In the past buildings were built using local time so the stones would wear their Sunday best for the whole week.

Supporters are weaving through the forest on their way home from the evening match. They are excited resigned or despondent. Each carries a faint glow from the floodlights into the darkness they will be home by the time the *News at 10* confirms them in their excitement resignation or despondency. Football is played all around the world because, as the man said, it is more important than life and death. It is also played locally so the nucleus of happiness is not jealous of scores.

Hence, a circle of insincerity lacks the diastolic and systolic use of words. The one thing we want our grandparents to be is dynamic *subsequently* when Peter and Penny waxed lyrical about the menstrual moon at least one of them knew what they were on about so I don't talk to trees but I do listen to them so and let them hug my heart while I draw their possession of a quality that could represent the very opposite of an arrogant languor. We are so jealous of this. We are greenery.

So a chrome crusader revolves faster at his poles than at his equator. This feature is the reverse of the sun and its gas giants the crusader's headlights pick out the *impossible terrorist* skulking at the border of the wood. He is impossible because he is turning right and left at the same time in a convincing version of executive power. The state is all powerful only to the extent that it can pretend it's licking its own eyes. So, spaghetti and indiscriminate moons. Class monitors at full tilt.

95. True

Is it true that a quiz show is morality free? The correct answer to this question is *Vertebra*. I'm gonna take a sentimental journey into the symmetry of truth. Grazed right knee then, following weeks of injury free hurtling down pavements, grazed left knee. Sometimes Radio 4 can feel unwelcoming an interminable middle-class dinner party but at other times it is *interesting and informative*. The truth of this has over two halves, yes, agree, flowery shirts certainly look good on some men.

The circle of sincerity is tacked on to a spiralling crisis. The motifs were heaped in a corner of a garden shed just as in late works Magritte piled his against the sky. These are toys just chucked there but the random arrangement enables the sizes to be compared although roughly equal the tunnel is the largest by the width of a room and the room the smallest by the length of a tunnel. The forest is made of Lego climbing through a lacrosse stick's net towards the rugby ball mannequin.

The circle is received into the truth. Another truth is conceived within the circle. A trompe-l'œil tennis racket press clamps an *artist's book* in the spacious white room above a table littered with small press grass mowers. This is the fortress of good luck in love. You follow a circuitous route that takes you behind every altar but never in front of one. You can hear a baby crying and water splashing there is chanting too or its mumbled apology. At the exit it must be mutedly closing time.

We made sure that our team covered as many subject areas as possible but as we were only three we could barely make a circle. Norman knew everything so that was handy especially if everything came up. Steve had rehearsed all the Treasure Island parts and I had added lyrics to my own songs fairly confident I'd recognize them in any questions if framed correctly in a relevant interrogation technique. Luckily we all knew the answer when asked the team name: *The Truth Brothers*!

96. Bet

Bet swiftly. Haggle at leisure. Don't look back unless you really want to very very badly. Check *now* then check *again*. If now has anything going for it it will let you know in time. Don't hassle. Let it sleep on it. Think less of your neighbour and a bit more of your foreign cousins. Choose a comic. Get on with it. I haven't got all day. I thought you didn't like that one. OK then. Don't blame me later. Bet slowly. Make the bookie bored with his honey. The horse is racing in your rented heart.

Wait swiftly. Another taupe jockey shirt. Another frumpy faux pas besmirching a diary jacket. Koons' Michael and Bubbles added to the periodic table. You can be anyone you want. No not that one. No not that one either. Sorry you can't be him. No you can't be her. Choose a different one. Look, how about this one. You really like this one don't you. Well you did. What's changed? Wait 'til we get back home. I'm going to hide you away. You can then wait as slowly as you like. Little bugger.

Engineering pandemonium. All bets are off. Poisons burn. Short poetic sentences. Long prosy sentences that talk about all materials having explosive potential and their day in the sun. That wasn't long. You didn't spend long on that. What's the point of doing it if you don't do it properly? The comic has two types of character, comic and seriously strong, heroically funny and evilly impelled. Then there's the scamp. Three types of neighbour. Too many cousins to consider, like insect bites.

A pillar of salt. A termite nest in the snow. A hotel collapsing making the strong look old and wrong. Another robot wrecking everything. Another painstakingly putting itself back together. Why couldn't it have mended that broken man who feeds the trees as if they were chickens. Every evening he even goes ten miles to put them away for the night then next morning goes to let them out. Race horses in the paddock watch, used to his passing. Steam is rising from the cuckoo's nest.

97. Miscellaneous

A miscellaneous vermouth modelled on a slight acquaintance with classical music chases down a not up to scratch Guinness in the Guildhall. Portraits of previous patrons line the walls each with a mitt in a bag of salted peanuts and a smear of chocolate across their chops: Loudon Wainwright III, Allen Ginsberg, Les from the Bay City Rollers, George Galloway, Bill Nelson, Sitting Bull and a stripper, Tony Benn. The jacket came off then he loosened his tie. Politics can be sweaty work.

Every pricey antique is surrounded on its table by miscellaneous items. The eye cannot take in all these little histories with one sweep. Sensing the vendor's eye assessing his and your immediate futures the effort of avoiding eye contact gets too much. You slowly meander to the next table, becoming miscellaneous again, until you pick up a brass woman being crucified for opening bottles. Before you know it you are saying *isn't this already mine?* but the stallholder has evaporated.

Padding and complicity. The mountain climber who wants to marry every new mountain he climbs finally gets engaged to a hydrogen cloud. The bridesmaids are his fellow climbers, roped together and all screaming silently in the blizzard. God is one dumb bastard. At the wake Pauline Fowler from *Eastenders* carries a tray of drinks with a forced smile that is nonetheless genuine. We are so glad to see her we forget our troubles and, discussing brown field sites, *force one back*.

The more trivial the gripe the more it will be followed to the ends of the Earth. A dissatisfied customer cannot distinguish ice from fire in their liqueur coffee and the car park at the ends of the Earth is even smaller than the restaurant car park. There are many channels of complaint to follow so the endlessly resourceful pair of detectives get out of the car and begin stuffing parcels into the nearest pigeon. Those of us preferring Coronation St. to Coriolanus don't know what comes next.

98. Unlimited

Unlimited sophist villa stone pushes a schooner below its plimsoll line. The trees climb the mountain but can go no further. Proto caribou. Promotion at a discount at all costs. Romans leave a mess full of messages the trees climb the sky but can grow no further. Having a crack at rendering the interplay of give and take in life and *elsewhere* entails having a shot at having a go at having a stab at it. Practise makes perfect homegrown versions of violence. Fledglings and counter weights.

Unlimited ice cream as long as it's vanilla empties out so a posse of rude brats go and hassle the waitress already doing the job of three to *refill it right now*. They want eternity to commence whereas the waitress wants it to condense. One dad of a brat goes to add his own brattishness to the harangue he seems to be happy about the situation as pleased as punch to be loudly demanding and boorish. We know what he votes, the party who vote for him. The waitress drops everything.

Orpheus wears a bathing cap and plays in goal for his water polo team. If he lets in unlimited goals they get fed-up so use his head for the ball. It was always cold watching, sat on the rickety top-tier of a wet two-tier bench. The game was being played in a pocket of dockside sea the pitch marked out with floating tram-lines ropes beaded with giant red and yellow beans refracting the thin evening light. I dropped my precious wooden skittle soldier. It rolled. It rolled over the dockside.

Sailors galore. Sailors galore haul Sandy Denny to safety. That twat in Pizzaland could afford to be dining with his brats somewhere a lot posher and he wants us to know it. That's what that little scene was really about. He was being sarcastic about the concept of the unlimited, displaying that weird form of patronisation that the ignorant rich employ with the world whether it be waitresses ice cream wild swimming or a befogged scree dipping its billion broken toes into the lake.

99. River 2

The river runs through the city because the city is only there because of the river. In one of the lockers in the lost property office an office block waits for its owner to claim it. It's been three years. The block doesn't know who its owner is. In the lobby a copy of the river leans against the reception desk. Is the woman behind it a receptionist? Is the uniformed man security? Are these tiny dolls citizens or are they subject to agency? River says to the city *let me just run through that again.*

We learn about loss but never learn how to lose things correctly *he's good but he doesn't do things properly* said my shorthand & typing teacher on the last day of childhood's open night she was from Lancashire she warned the girls about the bosses who'd be tempted by their short skirts but she didn't warn us boys about anything. She wasn't thinking properly. I took it to heart because I respected her opinion after all she did say my typewriter had a talent for creating strange tales.

The Forest Charter is signed by the barons on a picnic table – impervious blokes suddenly flooded with corporate scruples e.g. we can't say *Catherine wheel nipple* it's too easily said and *he's got a cathedral brain orf eggs* is easily tweaked too. If stuff was done properly it wouldn't have to be done by the book. All the charter needs now is a machine to read it with the correct headgear to wear for passing judgment. A Buddha made of chalky egg yoke is excavated from the office block.

It was not seeing the UFO his friend saw that did it for the *man* turning him into a narrator instead of a human being e.g. The Buddha of the Chalk Lands driving to a garage – he *fills up*. If you think he shouldn't get emotional you haven't seen him crying at a football match, filling the tank up with a fossilized conspiracy theory. UFOs come and go but a certain level of knowledge and competence is required when working in a garden centre, even if you're only responsible for the statues.

100. Desert

A desert adventure in the forest. Alive with the desert wind in your beard as you cross the city of dead trees in your jeep. As cruel as children. As brave as saints. A bit of a twat. A trickle-down rapist. As cowardly as saints. Mega fangled fantasists fed on holy shit and rolling news *me time*. The foggy foggy dew. Reduced sugar in the lap of a Duchess? Who's asking? Dead trees in your jeep. A remortgaged son. Litter lout rage. Due back at college 40 years ago. Viking jihad. White Irish teddy.

Sandcastles cannot be built on Chesil Beach or a week away at *The Golden Amber Forest Adventure Park* – Ionesco's rhino running amok in the Intifada. A childhood spent fighting wars of every description then given an Everyman *Leaves of Grass* by a bowler because of doing a good job unlocking the gates to the bowling green and tennis courts. In the same park one Sunday two foot under snow we (mum & me) arrived at Mass ready for anything: assassination, climate change, whatever.

Don't follow the yellow brick road follow the spam into big hairy gardens of the simple minded rich along with a big hearted wind blowing in their *hard earned* dosh but don't snatch just let the paper stick to your skin, a small compensation. Same scum lording it since 1066. Fuck 'em all. Recall Rufus Castle. Ivy rendering v power tools. Divert subversion. The caves beneath the old railway line at large in multilingual light. A quarrymen's picnic. Skull of Dêmos. Poison lager and lime.

When history takes a downhill bend too fast time travelling war reporters get off on watching battles there are too many to choose most opt for Passchendaele it sounds good or Goose Green it's far away but sounds just down the road where a feather and human heart still fall at the same rate as a sandbag an inside-out egg-timer the Jurassic Coast and writing giving rise to a type of *New Sentience* i.e. the Jurassic Coast is in a caravan overturning in a sandstorm of Tony Barrow prose.

Notes

The phrase *a democracy of poisons* appears in poem 17, 'Flock'. Following a reading in Liverpool it was suggested as the overall title by Joanne Ashcroft. I had written less than half the sequence at the time. So thanks Joanne.

Pg. 8 *Guitars made to resonate like bagpipes* – music of the band Big Country.

Pg. 9 *John Gray* – English political philosopher. Considered right-wing but whose thoughts can occasionally, and surprisingly, coincide with my own.

Pg. 14 *Peter Barlow's Cigarette* – reading series in Manchester named after a *Coronation Street* character.

Pg. 17 *Wally* – 'Where's Wally': series of children's puzzle books.

Pg. 20 *The DJ's mobile home* – a reference to Jimmy Savile.

Pg. 21 *Paradise* etc – a childhood fantasy world, Paradise being Weymouth. I kid you not.

Pg. 23 *Max Jacob* – French/Jewish poet (1876–1944). One of the finest prose poets and a huge influence on those who engage with this genre.

Pg. 25 *Vivian Stanshall* – Bonzo Dog Doo-Dah Band vocalist, died in a bed fire.

Pg. 26 *Charles Mintern and the Andy Jordanaires* – Put Nonism in your search engine, or The Listening Voice. Good luck.

Pg. 29 *slag slipped through the classroom windows* – The Aberfan tragedy.

Pg. 30 *I laughed so much at Tom's lines* – Tom Jenks – *I spilt my whiskey over a Welshman* – Rhys Trimble – *Aleksandr* saying *who took the custard ones?* – The Compare the Market meerkat.

Pg. 32 *Richard Barrett* – Manchester poet and friend.

Pg. 32 *Theme for an Imaginary Western* – song written by Jack Bruce and Pete Brown for Bruce's first solo album 'Songs for a Tailor'.

Pg. 34 *Christopher Priest* – my favourite SF novelist (see also Pg. 51).

Pg. 39 *Language Club* – reading series in Plymouth.

Pg. 48 *comet is made of comments* etc. – my first poetic experiments with surreal correspondences in 1968 were called *The Comet Comments*.

Pg. 52 *Out of Everywhere 3* – *Out of Everywhere* (1 & 2) are anthologies of linguistically innovative poetry by women, published by Reality Street.

Pg. 53 *Noye's Fludde* – opera for children by Benjamin Britten.

Pg. 55 *Barry* – Barry MacSweeney.

Pg. 56 *Some, sleeping in doorways, have been dead for two weeks* - I stole this but cannot remember who from or where.

Pg. 59 *Corbière's nauseous love affair* – Tristan Corbière, French poet (1845–75).

Pg. 61 *Li He* – Chinese poet (790–816) known for his poems of the ghostly and supernatural.

Pg. 62 *The Pranksters* – the Merry Pranksters and Ken Kesey etc.

Pg. 64 *Opposing Shore* – novel by Julien Gracq (see also Pg. 51). *Elementary Meanderings of the Trash Angel* – my unpublished first poems (1966). I imagined it having a sandpaper jacket, an idea that two years later was used in reality by the Situationists.

Pg. 74 *Bokononism* – fictitious philosophy/religion invented by Kurt Vonnegut.

Pg. 79 *Victoria Park* – park on Portland where I worked as a caretaker.

Pg. 84 *Oliver Ahern and Teresa Coakly* – Coakly, my mother's maiden name and Ahern, her mother's maiden name. Also pseudonyms for some reviews and poems in *Terrible Work*.

Pg. 86 *Allsorts* – a soft toy and close companion. He is supposed to be a panda but is more like a cat.

Pg. 90 *Nobody told me there'd be days like these* – John Lennon, 'Nobody Told Me'.

Pg. 90 *Murray Bookchin* – American ecologist and activist whose thinking was connected with libertarian socialism and anarchism.

Pg. 91 *Queequeg* – character from *Moby-Dick*.

Pg. 92 *none of them are on the line or know what any of it is worth* – Bob Dylan, 'All along the Watchtower'.

Pg. 93 *Certeau* – Michel de Certeau: French social philosopher (1925–1986). Quotes from his 'L'invention du quotidien' (The Practice of Everyday Life).

Pg. 94 *ship on a shipless ocean* – Tim Buckley, 'Song to the Siren' (see also Pg. 84).

Pg. 94 *Omaha* – Reference to Omaha Beach during the D-Day landings.

Pg. 97 *Green Army* – Plymouth Argyle FC supporters.

Pg. 101 *Norman… Steve* – Norman Jope and Steve Spence.

Pg. 105 *The Forest Charter* – A charter of 1217 returning to free men the right of access to the Royal Forests.

Pg. 106 *White Irish Teddy* – My teddy bear was one of many made in Ireland because in WW2 and for a period after, none were exported from Germany, where they usually came from. *Tony Barrow prose* – Tony Barrow was the Beatles' publicist and wrote album notes on the earlier LP and EP jackets.

www.ingramcontent.com/pod-product-compliance
Lightning Source LLC
Chambersburg PA
CBHW031635160426
43196CB00006B/435